NO PLACE TO HIDE

NO PLACE TO HIDE

The role of the banking Chief Operating Officer

A series of papers investigating the evolution of the COO in the new regulatory era

By Maurice Evlyn-Bufton

ARMSTRONG WOLFE
Executive Search

No Place to Hide; the role of the banking Chief Operating Officer
First published in Great Britain in 2017 by Armstrong Wolfe
Eagle Tower Suite 120, Montpellier Drive, Cheltenham,
Gloucestershire GL50 1TA United Kingdom
www.armstrongwolfe.com

Design and production: Rob Walster, Big Blu

For general information, please contact +44 203 664 8863 (UK) or email noplacetohide@armstrongwolfe.com

ISBN 978-1-5272-0241-2

CONTENTS

ABOUT THE AUTHOR

Maurice Evlyn-Bufton has over 20 years' experience in investment banking and global markets executive search and advisory. He set up Armstrong Wolfe in 2011 and has subsequently established the firm as a market leader within business management, more commonly identified as the office of the chief operating officer (COO), chief administrative officer (CAO), chief of staff (CoS) and, more recently, the chief control officer (CCO).

Maurice's quarterly industry papers and articles have helped establish his reputation as a leading voice in this evolving role of executive business management, supported by the quarterly COO and CCO forums he manages in London, New York and Toronto. These events are attended by 20 of the principal global banks and upward of 25 executives at each forum. He is supported in this endeavour by the team at Ernst & Young LLP. This has afforded Maurice a unique insight into this fraternity, enabling him to become a recognised authority on the subject and leading to the publication of two books on the subject: *No Place to Hide*, investigating the role of the banking chief operating officer in the new regulatory era, and *To Catch a Thief*, further investigating the evolution of the chief control officer.

Maurice continues to manage Armstrong Wolfe's day-to-day

business, working with his clients on global search mandates, having personally delivered retained searches in 25 countries since 2012.

He is a graduate of Cardiff University, which he completed through an Army scholarship. He attended the Royal Military Academy Sandhurst, being commissioned into the Gloucestershire Regiment. He saw service in the Balkans War, where he was 2IC of the British UN forces protecting the south bank of the River Drina, dissecting the safe haven of Goražde. He has returned to Goražde on several occasions and has raised funds through his charity (www.gcfbosnia.org) for the primary school in the town, in honour of his comrades who died in service in 1994–95. A book of his and others' reflections of their time in Bosnia, *Donkey Mail and Bully Beef: The Art of Survival* (*UN Operation Grapple, 1994–95*), will be available on a pre-order basis from summer 2017, with one hundred percent of its profits going to his charity.

Maurice is married to Joanna and has three sons, Simon, Monty and Alfie. He lives in the Cotswolds, England, and spends his spare time with his family, marathon running, mountaineering, walking his four dogs, writing and carrying out his charity work.

"Throughout the years I have worked with Maurice, he has continually demonstrated a unique perspective on the role of a COO and has prescient insight into emerging trends and issues within different markets. He is able to challenge convention and help guide COOs through the challenges we face; Maurice is a thought leader with vision and judgment."

MANAGING DIRECTOR, COO AMERICAS, SOCIETE GENERALE

"Insightful observations on the COO role from the man who has studied us the most."

MANAGING DIRECTOR, CREDIT SUISSE

"For a number of years the banking industry has undergone profound changes and COOs are at the heart of these changes. As with any industry, (e.g. automotive), new behaviours like cooperation are emerging, which are crucial for the survival of the industry. The merit of Maurice and his team has been to gather top COO representatives to begin this journey. A number of years ago, this may have been unthinkable."

HEAD OF CIB ITO BELGIUM AND HEAD OF BUSINESS OPERATING OFFICE OF CORPORATE AND PUBLIC BANKING, BNP PARIBAS

"Via the COO Forum, Maurice has supported the COO banking community in building a strong peer network. I have, personally, found this hugely helpful in terms of discussing common challenges and evaluating potential solutions."

GLOBAL MARKETS EMEA COO, CREDIT SUISSE

"I have known Maurice professionally for well over twenty years. He has always operated with the utmost integrity and has remained professional in his interactions and approach over the years in my various roles and in his. In recent years, he has played an integral part in trying to shape the debate in respect of first, second and third lines of defence; its definition, its place within the evolving capital market landscape, regulatory frameworks and the new norms of investment banking.

It is a huge testament that Maurice and his team have managed to assemble on a regular basis all of the key industry participants, both COO and across the Business Risk and Control functions, in order to discuss and address common issues and work together in shaping the future control infrastructures within the banks who participate.

This is coupled with trying to establish common ethical and behavioural training across the industry in order to raise standards and help firms retain and develop its talent. His global network in this regard is arguably one of the best in the industry. I've often sought his council on many topics affecting our ever changing landscape, and will continue to do so."

Managing Director, Head of Market Services, Commerzbank

"Maurice Evlyn-Bufton has a deep understanding of the unique role the COO plays within banking organisations and in particular how the role has evolved since the global financial crisis.
He has also been instrumental in creating a community within this group that has helped foster innovation and change within a dynamic market structure."

AT A GLOBAL BANK

ABOUT ARMSTRONG WOLFE

ARMSTRONG WOLFE
Executive Search

Armstrong Wolfe is a global executive search and advisory firm, focused on investment banking and the financial markets. Its main areas of expertise are business management, risk management, middle office and aligned technologies. Within these areas, the company has a reputation for sourcing talent with proven capabilities in driving change, be it responding to regulation or the institutional need to realise efficiencies and cost savings.

Supporting its executive search practice and responding to these transformational demands, Armstrong Wolfe provides interim and contract resource at middle management to senior executive level. Specifically, the company is recognised as an authority on business management, the roles of the COO, CAO, chief of staff, and chief control officer. The title may be the same company to company, but Armstrong Wolfe specialises in understanding the specific technical and behavioural skills required for success in the role and the ambiguities within the selection process.

This expertise and insight is framed by Armstrong Wolfe's quarterly COO and 3LOD Business Risk and Control forums, held in London, New York and Toronto. The global COO community faces market-wide and non-proprietary challenges, and acknowledging this, since 2014 Armstrong Wolfe has brought this community together to successfully investigate how best to address these challenges.

With offices in London, New York and Singapore, Armstrong Wolfe is able to meet the demands of its clients – some of the world's leading banking and financial institutions. The company strongly believes it has a unique insight into the challenges of the banking industry through its daily interaction with a COO executive network. Its forums have provided a platform for open dialogue that affords Armstrong Wolfe an exact understanding of the challenges facing the industry today, which has helped it build lines of confidence with its clients and candidates, whether they are from the front office or within the supporting infrastructure.

For more information, visit armstrongwolfe.com or contact info@armstrongwolfe.com.

OUR CHARITABLE CAUSES

This book will be distributed free of cost to individuals within the COO community.

One hundred percent of the proceeds raised from donations either at its launch events in London and New York, online or directly from this book itself will be distributed to our three chosen charities:

GCF Bosnia – gcfbosnia.org

Sightsavers – sightsavers.org

St. George's Society of New York – stgeorgessociety.org

For more information about the work of these charities, please see page 301.

If you would like to donate, please visit armstrongwolfe.com/charity and click the donation button to reach our JustGiving page.

For more information, contact us at noplacetohide@armstrongwolfe.com

Your donation is greatly appreciated. Thank you.

ACKNOWLEDGEMENTS

There are hundreds of people who have unknowingly contributed to this book through 20 years of client and candidate meetings. To all those who have offered their opinions, thank you!

Specifically, the counsel and support of the three Davids – David Ornstein, David Long and David Hudson – whose considered thoughts have been invaluable in helping me understand the subjects covered in this book. Similar thanks to Nick Lovett, Kevin Sawle and Toby Billington as guiding hands helping me navigate the subject of control and conduct and listening to me and my occasionally erratic, ill-considered ideas! Their support, thoughts and counsel have all helped frame the opinions and views outlined in these articles.

Thanks also to the members of my COO and CCO forums for giving up their time to attend my debates and adding colour and substance to the subjects I cover in this book.

Steve Krueger (Principal, Financial Services, Ernst & Young LLP) requires a special mention for prompting the thought that led to this book being published and supporting me throughout, and for his introduction to John Weisel (Global Financial Services Advisory Leader, Ernst & Young LLP). John kindly sponsored this book and secured both subject matter and editorial services from Ernst &

Young LLP, which has been invaluable.

Special thanks to Kate Owen-Dixon, my Marketing Manager, who dragged this book together, despite the frustrations and hurdles I lay down throughout its writing and production.

I would like to give specific acknowledgement to various publications that have helped to inform my writing: Nathan Bennett and Stephen A. Miles' *Second in Command; the misunderstood role of the Chief Operating Officer*, Vol. 84, No. 5, copyright 2006, and Jack Zenger and Joseph Folkman's *Are Women Better Leaders than Men?*, copyright March 15, 2012 (https://hbr.org/2012/03/a-study-in-leadership-women-do), both reprinted with permission by Harvard Business Publishing, all rights reserved.

In addition, former Royal Marines Officer and British Leadership expert Roderic Yapp's *The Real Reason the Military Works*, copyright June 16, 2016, was of help and interest to me (http://www.leadershipforces.com/real-reason-military-works/).

The Ernst & Young LLP report referenced on page 88, entitled *The DNA of the COO; Resetting the logic of the COO's role* can be found here: http://www.ey.com/gl/en/services/advisory/the-dna-of-the-coo---resetting-the-logic-of-the-coos-role.

All other quotes in this book were gathered anonymously from individuals within the COO community unless otherwise attributed.

To my wife Joanna, my biggest thanks, as she keeps me sane, has no interest or opinions on the role of the COO and by doing so ensures I keep all of this in perspective!

PREFACE

by John T. Weisel
Global FS Advisory Leader, Ernst & Young LLP

Over the past eighteen months, I have spoken with numerous chief operating officers (COOs) working within the banking and the capital markets sector, both in my role at EY and at Armstrong Wolfe roundtables.

I was interested to observe that these individuals fell – broadly – into two buckets: those who had been in the role for less than twenty months, and those who had been in the role for more than twenty years.

It may seem a curious observation, but it is one that goes right to the heart of the issues examined in this book: the evolving role of the COO in banking, and the personal and professional qualities those COOs need to succeed in their job.

So, why was there such a bifurcation in tenure?

In part, as this book shows, it is a result of the rapid and radical evolution of the COO role within the banking sector.

This is a role that is virtually unique to the industry. Despite the title being common elsewhere in the business world, where COOs are seen as heir apparent to the CEO, in banking it is a role that proliferates across the organisation, and is more of a counterpoint, or foil, to the CEO (or business head) than a replacement. They enable the CEO to focus on growth and strategy, by relieving the burden of regulation and change management.

As such, this book highlights how the role of the COO is as much determined by the strengths and weaknesses of the CEO as by any external factors. And the churn of business heads is a partial explanation of the bifurcation in COO tenure.

That said, the changing nature of the role itself is equally important. Over the last decade, there has been a radical shift in the role. Functionally, its scope has grown from planning and some control, largely in support of a pre-financial crisis growth agenda, to planning, control, risk and HR, with a major focus on compliance. The role and its responsibilities have increased, and it is now much more complex and important than ever. The COO bears real responsibility for what happens in the organisation.

It is a role that is likely to evolve again in the near future. A brief scan through the strategies of major banks shows a shift from a post-crisis agenda focused on control and protecting the enterprise – in essence, keeping the bank safe – to one about making things better, with optimisation and growth at its heart. It may be that, today, these strategies are more aspirational in nature – as banks struggle to escape the compliance agenda. But with the regulatory landscape crystallising, there can be little doubt that more banks will turn their thoughts to growth, and this will be yet another challenge to the skillsets of incumbent COOs.

The relationship with operations and technology rather than compliance will become core to the role, as banks look to build ecosystems, for example, making better use of "coopetition" (collaboration between competitors) or being more successful at integrating FinTech.

The combination of the relationship with the CEO or business head, and the evolving responsibilities of the role, hint at why so many COOS have been in post for a relatively short period of time.

Those who have lasted twenty years are likely to have been incredibly flexible. As this book highlights, by asking whether there are lessons to learn from military academies that might apply to the COO role, being able to adapt to new challenges is essential to success. From a bank's perspective, there is clearly more that can be done to recruit and retain a pipeline of successful COOs. One critical area to explore is gender diversity. According to EY's *Women. Fast Forward* initiative, we are more than 170 years away from gender parity, and in the COO space, women are underrepresented.

This book demonstrates there is more for banks to do to drive the equality agenda. Equally, it shows that banks need to ensure that they are not losing experienced talent by slashing headcount in pursuit of efficiency, and they need to consider greater collaboration.

This is the age of the COO. And yet the nature of the job is fluid and more complex than ever. It is critical that banks determine how they recruit, retain and retrain talent for these roles; key themes expounded on in this book.

I have worked with Maurice over the past eighteen months and during this time he has demonstrated significant insight into the evolving role of the COO. As such, I am pleased to contribute the preface to his book.

The views reflected in this preface are the views of the author and do not necessarily reflect the views of the global EY organisation or its member firms.

"The ambiguous nature of the business manager's role means that my views and conclusions have an equal likelihood of meeting with disagreement as agreement from readers."

PANDORA'S BOX

I set up Armstrong Wolfe in 2011, moving forward in a challenging market that was struggling post-credit crunch. With this fresh start, I decided to plough my furrow in an area I had only previously tiptoed in and out of, that of business management and the chief operating officer community.

It soon became clear to me that this community was both misunderstood and undervalued, but as we began to harvest opportunities, it became equally apparent that we were one of the very few beneficiaries of the new regulatory era. In this period, the COO moved front and centre, taking on responsibility for the tidal wave of new regulation. To manage this efficiently and effectively, there was clearly a need for additional headcount – and therein lay our opportunity.

By 2013, the business was doing so well that I set a further objective: to become the global number one for business management executive search and advisory for the financial markets. I can say with confidence that we are now regarded by many within our community as the authoritative voice on the role of the banking business manager: chief operating officer, chief administrative officer, chief of staff, chief control officer and all roles embedded in their offices.

This achievement has been facilitated in part by the series of articles I have written over the past few years, with the aim of gaining a broader and deeper understanding of the sector in which I work and the people within it – our clients and candidates. This book brings together those articles. It is a cacophony of COO conversations, a summary of the opinions of a large congregation of CAOs, the observations of CCOs and the mutterings of those who look into this community from the outside, trying to understand it.

The book's readership will be narrow, I expect: the business management community, maybe those interested in joining it, the occasional accidental reader, and my mother Diana (I promised her I would write a book one day, although I expect she hoped for something rather different).

The ambiguous nature of the business manager's role means that my views and conclusions have an equal likelihood of meeting with disagreement as agreement from readers. However, I always intended this to be a Pandora's box – not offering definitive answers but rather fostering thought and debate. If just one new person gains an understanding of the COO community and begins to appreciate the career opportunities and challenges it offers, then I will have fulfilled my aim.

Maurice Evlyn-Bufton
September 2016

UniCredit

"The question I have to ask is simple.' He spoke slowly, articulating each word carefully and clearly. 'What is the role … your role as a Markets' COO?"

IN THE BEGINNING - THE REGULATOR 2. NO TIME FOR POOR CONDUCT

A novel by Fed Libor

In a glass-walled room on floor thirty-two, high in one of the towers of Canary Wharf, East London, three people sat quietly. One Asian, one Caucasian and one Hispanic. Two men and one woman, a representative group of the diversity found within today's international banking sector. The two men were matched almost perfectly in dark suits, white shirts and lightly coloured ties. Alongside them a similarly well-dressed woman, also wearing a dark suit, differed in dress with a light-blue shirt. On the table before them rested their business cards, adorned with their company logos, contact details and names. Sitting neatly under each name was a corporate title: 'Managing Director, Global COO, Markets'.

It was a winter's day and the sun had set some hours before, which allowed the lights to shine brightly in the room, highlighting the freshwater blue colours of the carpet and walls. Outside, the lights of Greater London shimmered in the darkness. Close-up, street and office lights could be clearly seen, merging in the distance to be one soft, glowing orange-amber, iridescent mass of light. The three in the room were under investigation. The interrogator, the 'Regulator', shuffled his feet as he moved around the table, pausing to look out of the window and to the white, floodlit dome of The

O2 Centre on the opposite bank of the River Thames, before turning to speak to the trio.

'The question I have to ask is simple.' He spoke slowly, articulating each word carefully and clearly. 'What is the role … your role as a Markets' COO?' He raised his right eyebrow as if to further emphasise the succinctness of the question. 'More specifically, to what and to whom are you accountable? This surely can be answered by each of you equally and with brevity? After all, you are all presently in this role, as it states on your business cards. All three of you are working in global banks and are direct competitors within the same marketplace. I accept there may be some differences around the edges, but at its core, your roles must match. I would expect, therefore, some commonality in your answers.'

Again, he paused, waiting for a reaction, a response perhaps. 'From my perspective as your most beloved Regulator, your friend to keep you on the straight and narrow, you may say, I need to know for what you are responsible.' ('Or for what I will make you liable,' he thought.) He stopped, sighed and then his face twisted and turned to give birth to a self-congratulatory smile.

The three executives remained seated and silent in thought. This silence was only broken by the woman rolling her business card through her fingers from her left to right hand and back again, whilst she contemplated his words, gathering herself before speaking. She had pondered the parameters and the supposition of the question. They all knew that 'accountability' had become the Regulator's primary offensive weapon. This had been used with worrying regularity during its sustained assault on the banking market in the last few years, much of which all three would admit was needed and justified. But now it seemed that the cross hairs of attention rested on the Global COO. To the rest of the world, the title itself carried executive accountability, and therefore it was merely a process of painstaking analysis and debate to determine what this accountability should be, not whether it should be.

The previous assaults by the Regulator on the banking sector had left the industry reeling and gasping for air, wallowing in an apparent bottomless swirling pit of control and conduct policies and procedures. The by-product of these assaults was that CEOs had become accountable, with collective accountability rolling up into him/her. Conversely, lower down, individual accountability could still be allocated to a single person for their specific actions, but even here the CEO must have taken all reasonable steps to have prevented any event, as outlined in the senior managers' regime, to avoid accountability.

At COO level, however, where their mandates vary, this appeared to be difficult to determine. 'Why', you may ask? It was this well-known conundrum, this point of consideration, discussion and deliberation, that the woman mulled over before offering her reply.

'The same? You would think so – and understandably perhaps. Exact familiarity and comparisons between our roles, however, start and finish with the title. Am I a 'chief operating officer'? Yes, of course in title, but on a Monday I could be a COO, Tuesday a chief administration officer, Wednesday the chief control officer, Thursday chief of staff and by week's close stepping in as deputy CEO. I could be one or all of these, but yes, you could call me a COO.'

The two men nodded, acknowledging this summary and its recognition of the complexity and demands of the role they shared. 'I agree', one of them chimed in. 'My role, however, will be different from the other two, as my boss uses his COO – namely me – uniquely, as I daresay the others do too. It is my opinion that the personality of the CEO and his or her preferences on how the COO is used further defines the role, its mandate and influence.

More so, the capabilities and competencies of the person in the role are highly influenced by this circumstance, beyond the role specification carefully scribed by human resources to help identify this person, you may argue.'

The second suited man stood up, moved to the whiteboard at the far end of the room, his finger hesitating momentarily, hovering above the markers before opting for the black one. 'If you took a pie chart of time spent against tasks today, and we were to compare the chart to five years back or five years hence, the distribution of time and effort will be different … very different.' His hand galloped across the board, delivering shapes and forms remotely identifiable as pie charts. 'Whilst some tasks will remain constant throughout, such as budgeting, headcount and talent management, for example, others may not be found twice and some may have grown disproportionately over the interim period, such as …' he paused and looked to the other man standing '… regulation.'

The Regulator was now leaning on the small side table that appeared to be holding up an unfinished piece of modern art.

'There is no better example to support this hypothesis', the COO at the whiteboard continued, energised by the sound of his own voice and his moment upon the stage, 'than the progression of the role from pre-credit crunch, when the COO was enabling and supporting growth and looking externally, to post-credit crunch, when the COO's attention is internal and grappling largely with cost, control, conduct and regulatory challenges. At this moment, I feel I'm more de facto control officer, when I look at my in-tray, my inbox and my diary, than an outward-looking COO, tasked with driving the business, as I did some five years back.'

He quickly drew three circles on the board, adding a date below, 2005, 2015 and 2025. On the left-hand circle, 2005, he marked '10%', the middle circle, 2015, '50%' and the right-hand circle a question mark followed by the percentage sign.

'You see, our role shifts with the demands and requirements of the time. These demands may be commonplace, such as regulatory change, but may be unique, like managing a programme such as legal entity restructuring.' Under the three circles he wrote the words 'build' under 2005 and 'control' under 2015, and then added a further question mark under the 2025 circle. 'Take this the right way.' He looked directly at the Regulator, returning his smile. 'When we get to 2025 we all hope we will be spending far less time with you. Far, far less time and more time – a lot more time – on building and enabling the business, as we did in previous years.'

"You may be spending less time with me, I daresay this is correct, but those you are training to be the leaders of tomorrow and those I am training to be their regulators, are likely to be undesired bedfellows and will be jousting just as we do today.

"So, shall we continue…?"

This extract is satire, written by my fair hand, to capture the essence of the debate, the DNA of this book and frame the spirit of its narrative, as we seek to dissect and understand the mandate of the Markets' COO.

"CEOs and business heads have a valued resource within the COO and business management community, which has proven essential."

THE ORIGIN OF SPECIES

From 'nice to have' to 'must have' – the COO in ascendency

I first came across the role of 'business manager' when recruiting for Lehman Brothers in the late 1990s. At the time I was a partner in a new search business, Alexander Mann Global Markets, and up to this point in my career I had focused my efforts on middle-office and operations recruitment. I was approached by a client I had previously worked with when he held a managerial position within treasury. He had since been promoted into the front office into the role of EMEA chief administrative officer equities, and he now asked me to search for a VP business manager.

What struck me immediately was that this was unlike any other managed assignment, which were largely based on the directive of 'find me three or four people doing this role elsewhere and I will hire one of them'. Here, however, the client's opinion was that if this role did exist elsewhere in title, the person in the position would probably be undertaking very different tasks. I would, he directed me, need to find the person with an appropriate level of experience and particular competencies that could migrate into the role of the business manager. This wandering from the standard path was in itself a welcome break from the 'square peg, square hole' recruitment that had framed my daily activity since entering the world of banking recruitment in 1995, after serving as an infantry officer in the British Army.

The Lehman business management function proved to be a healthy artery of revenues and assignment opportunities up until its demise in 2008. However, it also put me on the path to further investigation and exploitation of this area of 'business management'.

Within this 20-year period (1995–2016), I believe there have been four phases of development for the business manager, who carries various titles representing a role with common and core responsibilities: chief administration officer (CAO), chief operating officer (COO) and in some cases chief of staff (CoS). Worldwide, the banking industry has liberally distributed these titles, with many banks having tens, if not hundreds, of people holding them. More recently, however, some banks have scaled this back to help define the seniority of the COO, CAO or CoS, retaining the title for one person (or at most four, if regional COOs are appointed: Americas, EMEA and APAC). Barclays, JPMorgan and UBS have all renamed COOs except the global COO (within markets) as 'business managers'. The four phases can be summarised as follows (see right):

Before the credit crunch, banking (specifically investment banking and the financial markets) experienced an unprecedented period of growth, although this later proved to be built on sand. During this period, few banks had an integrated or centralised COO function. CEOs and their business heads appointed a business manager to support them in the daily tasks of driving the business. Invariably this business manager reported to the business head directly, had no full or dotted reporting line elsewhere and was tasked, appraised and paid directly by the business. The role was generally unstructured and focused on facilitating and enabling growth, hiring the best people and directing capital investment into the support functions to ensure they could execute business support activities accordingly. The role looked externally, at new markets or new location opportunities, taking the vision of the business

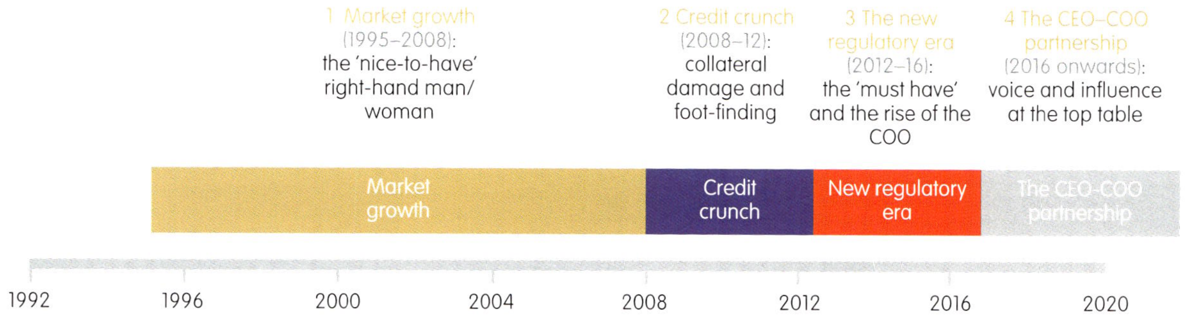
1 Market growth
(1995–2008):
the 'nice-to-have' right-hand man/ woman
2 Credit crunch
(2008–12):
collateral damage and foot-finding
3 The new regulatory era
(2012–16):
the 'must have' and the rise of the COO
4 The CEO–COO partnership
(2016 onwards):
voice and influence at the top table
Market growth
Credit crunch
New regulatory era
The CEO-COO partnership
1992
1996
2000
2004
2008
2012
2016
2020

head and new products and realising this vision. Of course, not all business managers carried all these tasks; some were more focused on budgetary management, talent management or managing the relationships downstream into the infrastructure. However, even in these cases, business managers were generally regarded as 'nice-to-have' resource, whose immediate proximity to the business allowed them to catch the portfolio of work more readily. They were generally left to manage the relationships on behalf of the business with such functions as middle office, operations and technology.

All these were of course business critical, but in an era of extraordinarily high revenues, they were not of interest to the business and so were often dismissed as 'back office', creating a 'them and us' culture. This approach gave rise to a generation of bankers, traders and salespeople who paid little attention to the importance of support functions, who were disparaging about their role and unaware of its complexity and burgeoning cost. To be king or queen in banking (or even a member of the high court), there was only one path to follow – a career in revenue production. A career *supporting* revenue production would never lead to greatness, although remuneration was still high compared to people with comparable education and skills in other industries.

At a time of high demand and when banks had money, they were struggling to hire and retain good people. One result of this was that even staff in comparatively low-skilled roles within core operations were paid handsomely, whilst middle to senior managers often earned hundreds of thousands and operations' heads into the millions, even though they generated no direct income for the bank. Not surprisingly, this uncontrolled wage escalation created a burden that has been carried forward to today. It is a resident item of consideration and focus for COOs and business managers, all grappling with falling revenues and fixed costs.

When the house of cards came down in 2008–09, it took the business-management function with it. In this period of bail-outs, restructuring and downsizing, the business manager moved from being a 'nice to have' to a 'not needed', as banks looked for ways of reducing headcount and streamlining activities. As a search industry, we experienced a steady flow of previously well-paid business managers now out of work. Growth and facilitating growth were no longer on the agenda, and as such, the COO, CAO and business manager were considered surplus to requirements.

For three or four years after this, the business management function was in the wilderness. Principal COO appointments remained in place, but the COOs and CAOs who had populated the broader business management function found themselves searching for a foothold to keep themselves in position or trying to find a role with a qualified mandate and purpose.

Some would argue against this suggestion, claiming that many COOs, CAOs and business managers remained in place, running the day-to-day activities of the bank, keeping the lights on and the wheels turning, even though they were struggling to hold an authoritative mandate while many business leaders fell around them. Even here, the COO remained largely invisible internally and externally amidst the turmoil.

It was only with the advent of new regulations, the by-product of the intense investigations and review into the banking sector post-2008, that the dormant roles of the business manager, COO and CAO emerged from their slumber. This was not marked by a quiet re-entry but rather a sudden step back into the spotlight. The COO's part in this new chapter unfolded quickly, and a well-defined mandate – a mandate of absolute necessity – was framed. In 2011–12, regulators issued a tsunami of new regulations, and the industry had to comply within specific time frames. Understandably, the regulators required this burden to be carried by the CEOs and the business heads, who needed to remain focused on revenue and wealth creation. What supporting role would help the CEO and the business meet these demands? The answer was simple – the COO, CAO or business manager. The business management function must be revived.

In this era, the COO partnered the CEO (and the business manager partnered the business head), executing the demands of the regulators. While the CEO and business heads retained accountability for all aspects of the business, the COO became responsible for ensuring it was being brought in line operationally. The CEO and business heads could thus continue to focus on delivering revenues in challenging markets, while their COOs focused their efforts on the control, conduct and governance agendas, to the extent that most banks subsequently appointed chief control officers (CCOs), reporting into the COO to bring a further focus on this business-critical area.

This hand-in-glove partnership brings together two people with very different skill-sets, but with a common aim. This is, in many ways, what makes the role of the COO and its relationship with the CEO or the business head and business manager unique to banking. The COO role is predicated on the need to meet these demands, and the skills to do so are framed by the book of work. It is very rare that COOs become a CEO, because they lack the prerequisite skills to perform this role, mostly associated with managing risk. At the same time, CEOs or business heads lack the skills and experiences to become an effective or accomplished COO, certainly in a stand-alone capacity.

By 2016, the role of the COO was defined by four principal areas of work, all framed by transformation and executing change:

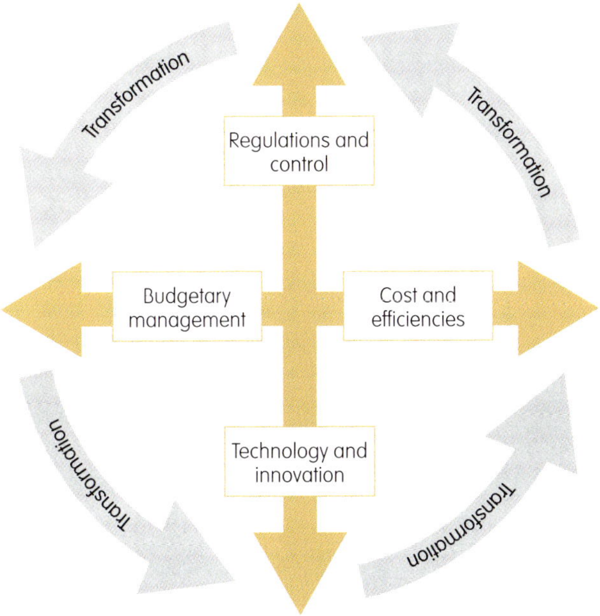

The challenge, of course, is allocation of resources and limited capital to deliver the change that will take the business forward, when presently the cost of meeting regulatory change, control and conduct consumes whatever capital remains. The skills required to be a successful COO are investigated later in this book, but it is important to mention the behavioural characteristics required to meet the demands of the role. Certainly these characteristics include an ability to thrive in a role embedded in ambiguity. It is equally important to have someone who is tenacious, yet possesses strong relationship management skills. This is not a job for someone who seeks an exclusive position in the spotlight, because the role will always be playing second fiddle to the CEO or business head. Much of what the COO does will not come to fruition for some time; indeed, the full implications of its value may not be realised until long after the individual has moved on from the role. There are few accolades for the COO, despite the weight of responsibility on their shoulders.

Four years into this regulatory transition, we see the first signs of a review of the COO role and the business management function. Additionally, the time, effort, resources and capital invested in building control teams (the first line of defence, 1LOD) would appear to be entering a period of interim maturity and consequent review, as banks look to adjust their models and seek more cost-effective ways of refining and enhancing the control framework. The market-wide 1LOD design phase has led to such conclusions and has been accompanied by innovative technology development, offering new solutions and choice. It is an interesting period that the COO community is entering.

Alongside continuing to captain and lead the control and regulatory agenda, the COO's role is now set on meeting new demands, driving innovation within the business and its infrastructure, or embracing technologies to retain and enhance competitive advantage externally. CEOs and business heads have a valued resource within the COO and business management community, which has proven essential. On one side, the recent ascendency of the COO has led to the role becoming more visible, responsible and influential. However, it is still not all-powerful. It has defined itself as a 'must-have' position but is still countered by the question 'What must I have?'

Some look at this position as a staging post to future promotion to run a business or even to become the CEO, taking a step out of a revenue role to do so. Where businesses are aligning themselves front to back and bringing technology and operations back into the business, the COO role is defined more fully as a bankwide, front-to-back, fully responsible and accountable executive position. The

COO sits on the executive board, but the role is unlikely to be a stepping stone to kingship.

It is in this period of further progression we find ourselves in 2016. Now is the time when the role of COO will develop, evolve and be further redefined. The new regulatory era bought the COO out of the shade and offered no place to hide, but conversely, as one of my clients stated, 'It could equally be read that the regulatory era offers no place to hide for the CEO, more so as it is the CEO and not the COO who is accountable.'

Perhaps then the marriage of the CEO and the COO within banking is one that brings together opportunity and necessity, where neither party can hide. An effective partnership between these roles is therefore essential in realising their own success – and the success of the bank and the investors it serves.

"Having returned to a business role, do you think having been a COO will influence your ability to be successful in your career in the future?"

THE ACCIDENTAL COO

From business to business management

"Historically the COO role was used to help administrate and support the business, executing the strategy and aligning the organisation to ensure it achieved these objectives. This is how I saw it, but having become one I can see how the COO role can be more effectively used. Its position affords the business head a chance to allocate a greater diversification of tasks, empowering the role and, by doing so, effectively making it the de facto deputy chair to the business"

(COO HEDGE FUND, PREVIOUSLY EQUITIES BUSINESS HEAD)

When completing the series of papers for this book, it occurred to me that most, if not all, of its content and opinions had been captured, harvested and framed by the interaction with my primary sources, the COOs themselves. This is understandable, a natural direction for my research to take, aimed at pulling together a well-versed narrative and argument, an informed insight to the role of the COO from those who live the role day to day, breathe its very existence and have mastered it to become successful in it.

However, despite the input from hundreds of information sources and countless number of conversations held on an ad hoc basis throughout the years and in the last twelve months, targeted and structured interviews, it felt something was missing. This quotation from a COO well known to me was the prompt, the moment that led to this reflection.

It firmed up my view that there needed to be some balance, a valued and respected outlook, an objective yet learned voice to offset the opinions of the COO, a voice that would hopefully complement their narrative. Otherwise, it could be argued that this series of papers was a narrow self-assessment, an insular consideration of what this *band of brothers* does and how COOs see themselves. At worst, a self-congratulatory play, a libretto reaffirming the complexities and demands of the role and a cry for those who underestimated it, to understand and appreciate it.

Who could offer this insight with the required and informed fairness? Who else than those who assess COOs' performance, appraise them, rely upon them and in doing so are an authority on them. Those who have managed them and more so, those from this group who have been both a COO and have run a business using a COO. This managerial view was absent, being the assessment by those who had used and partnered a COO, it was their opinions that would make my assessment complete. I turned to one such contact and asked his initial thoughts on the subject, hoping his reply would support my thoughts:

> *"It's a fundamentally different job than the one I had anticipated. There is a never-ending list of tasks, actions and decisions to be made. This level of diversity is matched only by the ever-changing priorities of the role and shifting timeframes. I often*

came into work with a well-planned and framed mindset to grapple with the tasks that lay ahead of me that day, for this plan to fall PRT almost as soon as I entered the office. I would immediately have to switch priorities to a new event of business criticality that had superseded and overrode all others. It is having this understanding that things change every day, that your COO never tells you 80% of what they are doing, that you appreciate once you have been in the role itself. It must be an ever-present temptation for a COO to want to tell their boss what they had been doing that day, that week or month, to allay any concerns that may be festering as to 'what does my COO actually do to keep occupied daily?' Plenty, I'd say, more than plenty, I can say that from experience."

Another added:

"The effectiveness of the role is the holy trinity of the CEO to COO relationship, requiring the right person in the leadership role, giving the role its empowerment - a well-defined and constructed mandate, playing to both strengths and interests and the right person, with the right behavioural characteristics and aspirations in the COO role. Get these three right, and business as a whole

will be the beneficiary of this well-honed and executed partnership. In turn, your effectiveness in the role rests on how you use the authority of your manager and how your manager has communicated he or she is happy for you to use their voice. People in the organisation need to understand and take on board when the COO calls, the call and the request or order have come from the CEO and, as such, need to be dealt with accordingly. This is an art in itself."

Herein is a managerial group that would offer the necessary insight into how a COO role is perceived by those who directly rely on them. Linking in with this group would enable me to gather their thoughts as to what they think makes the COO role effective, thereafter to establish the profile of the person they require and from those who have been a COO and used one, what was discovered by taking this career path:

"Having been a COO and returning to a position running the business, I am now far better equipped and positioned to lead this business. Why? I had underestimated the diversity and volume of tasks addressed and managed by my COO. I have also become acutely aware of the demands and intricacies of the regulatory agenda and have been exposed to the full cost of running the business from front to back and,

perhaps equally, the organisational challenges presented in getting things done and moving the change agenda forward. Having this knowledge makes me a better business head and allows me to carry the burden of regulatory responsibility more readily, more comfortably."

This quotation is somebody who had been on the journey to be a COO and back into the business. We discussed his thoughts when he was presented the option of moving, not just from running a desk to being a COO, but a move organisationally from one bank to another, from a principal U.S. investment bank to a U.K. bank:

"It wasn't a move I had thought about until presented the option, as the role of the COO at the bank I was employed was more akin to a CAO and business manager supporting you, rather than driving the business effort in partnership."

He went on to explain:

"It came down to four things:
1. What did the hiring manager see as the role of the COO?
2. How aligned was his thoughts to the role of other COOs embedded elsewhere in the markets' division?

> *3. Did I trust in his statement to make good on the mandate as outlined?*
> *4. Who paid me - my boss and the business or was it from a COO centralised pot?"*

In this case he was well known to the hiring manager, so what could be the hardest judgement call to make was actually the easiest, as trust was established from previous years of working together:

> *"It was clear to me his view of the role was I would be his de facto, but not stated, deputy. In this capacity, by attending meetings on his behalf and by him always supporting me and the decisions I made, I felt it to be a good fit to how I saw the COO role operating. He was not the sort of person to allow manufactured corridor conversations with him, aimed at diluting my authority, by those seeking to avoid such points being channelled through me. This in itself guaranteed the role had empowerment and influence."*

"This is all to the good" I said, "but what appears in your case is a relationship based upon trust, and this trust takes time to be established":

> *"Yes of course" he countered "but the manager must have an explicit understanding of what the COO role is, its mandate and how he or she*

intends to use this mandate. I always kept my boss up to date with matters, speaking daily, many days on an hourly basis on various issues. Over time, through effective communication, trust is built, and you both work out the parameters of your responsibilities. I would never make a decision that I wasn't 100 per cent confident my boss would support and/or would make himself. This takes time, but can only be established by having a high level of trust from day one, regardless of whether you are known to each other beforehand. This is underpinned by a trust explicit in the mandate and authority of the COO position."

What, therefore, had been learnt from this experience? It was clear from our further discussions that he had carried forward into his new business role the importance of communication, ongoing and effective consultation and the simple need to make time for your COO, regardless of the level of trust that exists between you. Additionally, never to undermine your COO or the COO's position and mandate, as the greater the level of empowerment you give it, the more you can leverage from this position:

"Understanding your role can depend on the line of authority, ownership and influence on how you manage your time. Understanding the influence and power gifted to you by your manager is equally important and how you learn to use this

empowerment. It is not just a matter of who signs your appraisal or who pays you. You need to understand where your role sits in the psyche of your boss and the company as a whole. Ask yourself the question: How often do I speak to my boss, the business head, as opposed to how often do I speak to my boss, the functional and global COO? How much of my time is taken up on tasks being delivered from either party? This balance is a pretty clear indication of where your role sits in the organisational structure, despite what you may think or feel."

I pursued this angle with another business head and previously appointed COO who appeared to support this statement. "One aspect I appreciate, having been a COO and now having one myself, is that if you hire the right person into the role, who will almost undoubtedly be of higher calibre than what you would have hired prior to me being a COO, you can use this role to greater impact and effect. Only, however, if you empower the role and its position."

However, what can impede this process is the organisational alignment of the business management function and what is the role of the COO within it, which is defined by the bank and not the individual business heads.

"Yes and no" one former COO commented. "Ultimately, in whatever organisational construct, I would find it surprising, if not untenable, for a COO to be imposed on a business head without his or her vote of confidence. In fact, the business head being the final vote on whether he or she should be appointed COO is a given, I would suggest."

This is where the demands of the business are occasionally in conflict to that of the parent organisation on such matters. What the business sees as the role and, therefore, the person fit for role may well differ from what the bank understands as the role of the business management function and, within it, the role of the COO, CAO or business manager.

"How would you define the differences between these three roles by title?" I asked a COO who had been a COO at one bank, a business manager at another and now was seeking to hire his CAO:

> *"The Chief Operating Officer (COO) – executive appointment to the head of a business, executing the strategy on behalf of him/her and tasked with managing all aspects that enable it to operate effectively, in a controlled and cost-effective manner. The Chief Administrative Officer (CAO) – all the above, different title Business Manager (BM) – both the above, different title. For good order, I would add the Chief of Staff (CoS) – the intellectual sounding board of the head of the business, his/her moral compass and go-to person on all matters that may well fall into one of the above and all other aspects. A role without portfolio, but weighted heavily with influence."*

This summary captures the thoughts of several business leaders and CEOs, expressing the frustrations that are caused by changing titles and expectations set by such titles at different companies:

> *"In my opinion, most COOs today are in fact CAOs, as their time is taken in enabling the business to operate from an operational and administrative perspective, as opposed to supporting and defining strategy, product development and growth."*

This is a fair comment, but one that came from a business head who had not been a COO or CAO or indeed business manager and not surprisingly saw the role through a lens that had predefined limitations as to the role's capabilities and influence. Another added:

> *"There are core areas of commonality from one COO role to another or, in our case, from one business manager to another, but ultimately it comes down to how you as the business head want to use and empower your COO, CAO or business manager and understand how this position and person can be used. What you must do is meet the external and internal demands of the regulators and the CEO's office, respectively, where you can become a COO in name and in deed and yet move to be a business partner and deputy, if you look beyond this limited mandate."*

What came through from many of my conversations was the challenge facing the business and their COO in building a steady state, in relation to communication and information requirements:

> *"As a COO I have realised, you spend a lot of your time dealing with day-to-day issues, tasks, responses, that as the business head you really have little time or, fair to say, interest in hearing about. Effective communication fills this gap adequately, communication in all its facets and directions."*

How the CEO or business head communicates to the broader population regarding matters pertaining to the COO and the COO's office will be key to framing the mandate and influence of the COO. It becomes very clear and visible quickly whether a business head has confidence in the COO or CAO and how this position is viewed from the top. This perception can be shaped in open conversation and dialogue amongst senior management, or through official communications from the CEO's office or, more so, the level of representation the business head affords the COO in representing them at various committees.

The question is whether you as the COO feel you can generally speak with the authority and on behalf of the CEO, to your business head. The acid test is a clear demonstration as to whether the CEO backs the COO at all times, be this when being lobbied in the corridors of power or when sat at a round table together or when the COO makes a questionable or poor decision. What is required with the last point is a deep-rooted understanding of the supporting role of the COO by his or her manager and strong personal and leadership characteristics of this person to manage through such a scenario with calmness and objectivity. Naturally it depends upon other factors, but if such errors of judgement are infrequent or unique, and not singularly unforgiveable, the test for the COO will be at the point the person makes his/her first mistake and how this is handled by the business head or CEO:

> *"Communication is key to the success of the role, where the COO acts as if a bolt-on server to the CEO. The way the two of them work together must appear seamless, a united voice of authority and action, where the COO must be empowered to represent the CEO in multiple matters and, by doing so, allowing the CEO to focus on the critical business decisions and strategy. By taking this mandate, the COO must work hard to ensure the CEO is never blind-sided by any decision made for him or her and must act as the bridge between the employees and the CEO, ensuring groundswell and core opinions are communicated, understood and, if required, addressed by the COO on behalf of the CEO (or the CEO alone). The more controversial or impactful the issue or decision, the more important the need to have open access and communication between the CEO and the COO, allowing a meaningful conversation, sometimes at very short notice. Limits of such authority will change in time, as trust and understanding is built, where the essence of the success of this two-way*

relationship is based upon the simple principle of effective and respected communication. If the CEO does not recognise this and does not make time for the COO or respond in a timely manner to the COO, the foundations of the relationship are put under pressure, and the mandate and influence of the COO role will be diluted."

The challenge, therefore, as a COO, is what level of information do you deliver to your manager, because in part and it is natural to do so, you wish him or her to know what you have been dealing with on their behalf on a daily basis:

"You are conscious that your boss expects you to deal with the minutiae and execute on the never-ending 'to-do' list born out of the daily requirements to run a business in good order. There exists an understandable temptation, however, to tell your boss too much, to avoid the accusation or rather the question of 'what keeps you busy all day?' and, indeed, to avoid the potential issue of being overburdened with tasks and work from a lack of understanding of the workload being managed. This has become an issue for some business lines, which are clearly under-resourced, due to the focus on cost, but retain an absolute requirement to meet the changing parameters of regulation."

Here again communication, or rather education, was cited by a number of business heads as being important in getting this balance right, in ensuring your manager is kept up to date with your efforts and the tasks at hand, whilst not overburdening him or her with unnecessarily granular detail:

> *"If I had not previously been a COO, I would have not grasped the challenge and the demand on resources and, importantly, the time that my COO and the COO's office needs to deal with today's intense programme of change, driven by cost and regulation. In this context it is a fine line between effective and needed interaction as opposed to over-communication which must be established. It is fair to say it rests with the business head to establish and define the right level of information needed to meet your demands. To not do so could possibly cause unneeded tensions. In summary, simply do not underestimate the pressures of the to-do list: this is my takeaway from my experience being a COO."*

This point, the diversity of tasks, its endless demands and the ability to manage them effectively, was a common point made throughout my investigations. This was invariably partnered with an insight and comments as to the skill-set of the team needed under the COO to meet these demands:

"What became immediately apparent was the challenge in managing multiple deliverables and meeting the daily, monthly and ad hoc tasks of the business. More so, how to do so with a small head count, where you are constantly challenged to do more, better with less, as the pressures of change and cost cascade into the COO's office. The unfortunate meeting of shrinking revenues with the burden of regulation and cost management have found a home in the COO's in-tray.

My first month in the role was a shock in context to the expanse, variety and importance of the decisions left to the COO to handle. It was as if the COO's in-tray was the backstop for all decision-making, big or small, for the head of the business and the business as a whole. Perfecting the art of delegation was an immediate skill-set called upon, just as developing an understanding of the capabilities of the team below you that was needed to delegate accordingly.

You need to have a diversity of people within your team, matching the diversity of the tasks to be managed and delivered. You need someone that thrives on the 'here and now', the immediate task framed with ambiguity, just as you need the more thoughtful person to take on a strategic view on a mid- to long-term deliverable. You need the team to complement your own short-comings; you all need strong influencing skills, and you will need someone detail oriented and accurate, just as you need someone that will never say 'no' to a task and someone that is guaranteed to ask 'why?' You need an in-team diplomat, and you need the reliable all-rounder. All of them need to understand their careers rest on visibility and their delivery, not on a pre-defined journey. You need above all to be able to build, motivate and mobilise this team to be a successful COO."

Most agreed from within this select group that the COO role appears to have evolved recently in its seniority, to meet the diverse and evolving demands of the banking sector. It was felt its position has certainly benefited as business heads have trafficked through the role, giving it visibility and a greater level of understanding. As they have done so, they also develop an understanding of how the COO position can be used more effectively, where to do so it invariably requires an upgrade in the calibre of person manning the battlements.

Additionally, it was felt from this targeted group that the demands of the role today supported the businesses desire to seemingly over-hire into a COO role, doing so when the agenda was clearly to upgrade and to bring additional capacity and impact to the position. The challenge taking this route is to find someone who is happy to deal with the diversity and breadth of the role's responsibilities, from being the go-to person for all tasks, however menial, to acting as the CEO in waiting or holding the seat of the CEO in absence.

The incentive to secure the attention of the best people to take such a choice is very much captured by that word *career*. The COO role is increasingly seen by many as a career enhancing one, a move to be made by choice and one that is understood to give the foundations of mid- to long-term career opportunity. In doing so, revenue-generating candidates are increasingly found seeking out such opportunities, internally and externally.

This interest may be shown by a business personality looking to benefit by migrating through the COO role (and back again). However, for some who take on a COO role with this same intention, the end result can be very different. It is not uncommon that some find the role and what was supposed to be an interim move more demanding, more rewarding and empowering than previously thought likely, and as a consequence some do not return to a business role. I know of cases where none-too-enthusiastic entrants to the COO world have unintentionally set their career path within business management. This finds them sitting alongside COO and business management career professionals, who have not come from a business, sales or trading background, who are perceived as being very different in experience, qualifications and personality, but are equally thriving in its multiplicity and variety, "The COO and business management function would lose its balance and strength, if it did not have the mix of both", one COO commented.

I asked the question of one senior business head, "Having returned to a business role, do you think having been a COO will influence your ability to be successful in your career in the future?" The response was immediate:

> *"Totally, I understood this at the outset and is exactly why I took the role. It has given me a breadth of skills and experiences which are*

more transferable and will, I am sure, create opportunity in the future, perhaps in and outside banking. You don't have to be a master of all tasks as a COO, but you must master being a COO itself; then you can take this experience forward into your career to your advantage."

"Explain this point more" I asked:

"I believe upon reflection, what I have learnt about being a COO, and therefore what I will use when hiring a COO, is you don't have to be 10 out of 10 in everything. A COO who is 7 or 8 out of 10 in most things, perhaps with one or two areas of high competence, will succeed in the role and be well matched in overall skill-set to do so. You need to understand this as a business head and need to understand the COO needs to hire against their skillset to ensure as a team, as a collective, that the team is 10 out of 10 in all areas."

"A COO will find the moment to excel and move from the periphery to the heart of the business"

REDEFINING THE ROLE

The COO post-credit crunch

The principal responsibilities of the COO were established in response to the demands on business heads to have a reliable and senior resource at hand to deal with the myriad challenges and tasks they faced in relation to personnel, budget, operational processes and technological requirements. In many commercial organisations, these tasks are often more commonly allocated to the Chief of Staff (CoS), Chief Financial Officer (CFO) and Chief Technology Officer (CTO). However, within investment banking, the front-office or product COO evolved to respond to specific and often unique demands within areas that had arguably become stand-alone businesses – with significant revenues – in their own right.

The COO title is common, but the multitude of responsibilities allocated to it varies widely between individuals and institutions. The point of evolution of a business, its regional footprint and the personality of the COOs themselves will often inform the mandate of the role. This may fluctuate from being a fully empowered executive, driving the business forward, outward looking and in partnership with the business heads, to being a COO in name, but in practise acting as Chief Administrative Officer (CAO). This role is limited to coordinating and delivering a host of administrative and operational requirements, enabling the business to maximise sales and trading effort.

A fully empowered COO will invariably carry the full weight of a CAO's responsibilities. This catch-all dynamic has become increasingly common, with tasks that are highly administrative in nature, being regulatory, compliance, and control issues, becoming business critical and are now central, not periphery, to the main effort of a COO. The absolute nature of these tasks makes them a priority on the agenda of any COO. This has, therefore, shifted the weight of a COO's responsibilities more towards the administrative. Why? The catch-all has long been part of the COO's mentality ('We do whatever's thrown at us') and it has been both its enemy (making it difficult to quantify the role) and, more recently, its saviour, delivering influence and a degree of power.

What one COO does for his or her business head can differ greatly from another. Such variation offers challenges when benchmarking performance, value and reward. 'I know the value they bring to me' carries limited weight in an era when being able to quantify value is paramount. One result of this ambiguity was that COOs were often casualties in the post-credit crunch cost-cutting period. It is easy to understand why. A COO does not directly contribute to revenues so naturally became the target for headcount reduction or at least compensation compression.

A new era

Some COOs do in fact define the CAO as the 'Catch-All Officer'. For many this carries a negative connotation, but for some it has manifested itself in positive ways. The market shift in relation to regulation and the new focus on control (both cross-product, market-wide and product- or business-specific) – and the responsibility to deliver on both – have become part of the COO's mandate. What was aligned activity and responsibility has become central and absolute. COOs are now burdened (some would say overburdened) with the tasks born of these requirements. Where headcount in the COO's office was previously scrutinised, many now find a request for increases in this area favourably received. This has enhanced the role of the COO's and their visibility across the business front to back. It will be the making of many and the fall of some.

The regulatory and control era offers the opportunity for the COO community to define itself as critical to business success. What has been a nebulous mandate in the past is evolving into one that is clearly defined and business essential. This will, of course, change the allocation of time and effort expended on the daily, monthly and yearly tasks of the COO. The current COOs, whose experience has been weighted to the traditional deliverables of the COO (growth, building, strategy, etc.), will have to adapt to the demands of today (control, cost, efficiencies). It demands that the COO addresses this skill-set shortage or exposes the function or people within it to being replaced or 'upgraded'.

Some say that 2011–13 was the dawn of a new era for the COO and an opportunity for those whose profiles may have been previously unsuited to the role. It was inevitable that the profile of the COO would change, as the market demands a different skill-set and where the responsibilities of the COO will likely become more quantifiable in the future, required through regulatory responsibilities or by the growing cost of the COO function.

The by-product of this change will be enhanced and visible responsibility and increased accountability. It is possible – even probable – that COOs and their CEOs will have imposed and enhanced regulated responsibilities regarding control oversight and will be held responsible for control errors. Extending this supposition, it is not beyond the realm of possibility that regulators may seek to legislate this responsibility and allocate collective accountability to the most senior business people. "A Sarbanes-

Oxley for the COO role would make many think carefully on this as a career path", one COO commented.

Such a shift would also change the demands for reward, although it is currently accepted that this responsibility and that of trading risk and failings within the trading environment, rests with the business heads rather than the COO. However, many argue the COOs should 'feel' they have this accountability to ensure that risk is managed and mitigated appropriately, even though business heads retain accountability. Such accountability is presently self-regulated and internal as opposed to external and imposed. It is unlikely that this situation will remain, as the creeping regulatory agenda will shift its lens to this area. However, one common view is that the COOs should be rewarded consistently across businesses, where individual performance assessments will be closely aligned to the success of managing control and operational risk within their area of direct responsibility.

The industry as a whole is being made more accountable, and in these changing times the COO will find the moment to excel and move from the periphery to the heart of the business.

The changing profile

The change in focus of the COO has increased the importance of the role. In doing so, it threatens to alter the weighting of the role and, consequently, the profile of person appointed. Presently, the COO community is largely populated by ex-traders or product controllers. The new regulatory and control era demands a COO with a broader background, perhaps including experience in legal and risk management.

The responsibilities of a COO and a CAO can be split, allowing the technical and behavioural competencies required to be individually defined. As the list of deliverables grows deeper and wider, the criteria required from a successful COO becomes correspondingly broader. The COO will be faced with the dilemma of working to retain these integrated responsibilities and, most likely, requiring additional headcount to deliver them or having to distribute some to support functions. COOs will maintain a dotted line of responsibility to ensure delivery, so while they may lose some control, they will retain responsibility and accountability.

Stripping out some of the traditional responsibilities leaves those that are core and business critical – the principal demands that will define the experience of the COO in a new era for the banking industry. This will of course vary from bank to bank and from product to product, but business heads will be required to think carefully about the primary responsibilities that should be laid on the shoulders of their COOs. In doing so, they will have to think more deeply about the skill-set required to deliver those priorities.

"The interrelationship of the CEO and the COO is essential to the success of the business."

PLAYING SECOND FIDDLE

The mandate and profile of the front office business manager

Executive summary

The evolving role of the COO – how its mandate is defined, its tasks allocated and executed, and the nature of its growing internal and external accountability – is a subject of debate across the banking community. Historically, the role was tied to a business and not necessarily a person. Invariably the COO stayed in place, providing continuity for a business as leaders were anointed and then lost their crowns. While this has changed with time, today some COOs still prefer to be the power behind the throne – the consigliere, if you will – while others embrace the opportunity to step into the limelight that the evolution of the role has offered.

Changing demands in the market have forced banks to look at this important and well-paid resource, delivering a change in the mandate and empowerment of the COO. The need for enhanced communication and greater accountability, as well as a continued demand for cost reduction and coordination of the control and regulatory agenda, has led most banks to centralise the business management function, be it within the business itself or into finance. This is no simple undertaking, as organisational, business, regional and personality nuances have left the industry with a single reference point for this role: the title 'COO' itself. Many argue that this title is overused, misunderstood and diluted.

The move to a centralised COO (business management) organisational structure is one many believe in, and it lies at the heart of this discussion. It may appear that we gloss over the current debate regarding the complexities of pay (or overpay) within banking, which in the case of the business management structure is further complicated by matrix managerial structures and the sometimes unfathomable and inconsistent allocation of financial reward. However, we have assumed here that within the business management function, the issue of cost can be resolved and savings realised for the shareholder by avoiding overstaffing and overpayment in administrative roles such as junior COO, business manager and support staff. Such roles can be overpaid when funded from the front-office compensation pool, when this headcount could be moved into the infrastructure or, as this essay argues, moved into a centralised pool where performance and reward can be evaluated objectively. We do not seek to interrogate the compensation agenda, but refer to it only in context of the question under consideration – defining the role of the COO.

However, there is one argument regarding business management compensation, supported by many COOs, that is worthy of note here. Since investment banking as an industry has hit a plateau – or even shrunk – as both ability and appetite for generating new derivative products has declined, the value-add of certain internal banking functions needs to change. Some argue that low- and mid-level front-office staff are joining established global banks with existing customer bases and should not receive inflated compensation relative to other industries. A comparison might be a junior lawyer joining a top ten law firm, a trainee accountant at a top four firm or an associate at a leading consulting firm. All these industries compete for the best talent and do not use compensation as a primary recruitment tool. The best people are enticed by future opportunities and a well-trodden path to seniority or partnership.

Conversely, it is possible to contend that it is the COOs who are now adding long-term value in banking by creating and establishing new workflows, which adapt to new regulations in a cost-effective way. Some would state with confidence that the experienced and proven COOs who get this right for their firm are worth significantly more than a global asset franchise trading head whose mainstay is one-year-at-a-time client revenue generation. This matter will always be an emotional and personal one, especially when change is proposed, and opinions surrounding it are not always linked objectively to the benefit of the company.

More recently, compensation has been married to control through the conduct agenda. In this regard, it is possible to argue that the benefits of mobility and consistency outweigh the loss of management control by business heads; there appears to be no substance to the argument that a central COO function cannot retain a close business alignment when not owned by the business. Equally, this alignment delivers a degree of objectivity and independence to the relationship. Regardless, it is rare for a business manager to be drawn cross-product, although it is common for people to think in this way. This may be good for the company, but it is irritating to a business that wants to maintain a silo mentality. Some companies have both a central team and a business team, and the passage of time has shown that sometimes this works and sometimes it does not.

It is my contention that the banking industry has created confusion and a problem of individual empowerment through the dilution of the title 'COO'. We can contextualise this by a loose comparison with the same role in other industries. Outside banking, most corporates have a single COO, and all employees know this is an executive role that carries significant weight. In contrast, most banks have dozens – sometimes hundreds – of COOs. Why? This may be a throwback to the heady days of growth and profitability, a historic extension of the ego of the business heads ('I have a COO') rather than reflecting a genuine need to empower the role through the connotations imbued within the title, chief operating officer. It has even been suggested that banks have used it as emotional compensation – promotion by title, not by mandate. Some banks are addressing this, replacing the title of CAO or COO with 'business manager', but even here 'COO' continues to be used in general parlance and along the corridors of investment banks. In fact, the list of responsibilities outlined for a COO supports the migration of the title to CAO, whereas in most non-banking companies many front-office banking COO responsibilities would fall within a CAO or CFO role. For example:

- Working with the head of the business to set and drive product/divisional strategy: COO (or Head of Strategy where one exists).
- Coordinating and driving the product business managers/COOs under management towards business objectives: COO (responsible for the execution of the strategy).
- The control, conduct and governance agenda (front to back): COO (or Chief Control Officer).
- Coordinating the support functions and management of the front-to-back business line and offering: COO (a portfolio of work more aligned to a CAO).
- Reporting on and monitoring the use of the business's weighted risk assets and external assets and managing its 'financial capital': CFO.
- Reviewing and managing the capital of all subsidiaries within the sphere of the business: CFO.

- Setting and managing budgets for the business: CFO.
- Collective responsibility for capital management, including profit repatriation, capital hedging and the closure of dormant subsidiaries and legal entity restructuring to establish more efficient capital utilisation and business management: CFO.
- Collective responsibility for driving effective capital management throughout the organisation, establishing guidelines and budgets with the business for balance-sheet usage, and monitoring adherence to those guidelines and budgets: CFO.
- Managing transformation and change within the business and its support functions: COO (CAO core tasking).
- Responsibility for staffing and talent management: HR.

"The interrelationship of the CEO and the COO is essential to the success of the business."

In brighter times, this list would have included developing new products, opening new markets, starting new businesses, etc. These lie at the heart of any true COO's responsibility to drive revenues. However, today these more positive aspects have been replaced by setting up governance and control frameworks and responding to ongoing regulatory demands, pulling the COO into a CAO's framework of tasks.

It is possible to review the weighting of the COO's book of work at any time and state that the person is now operating as a CAO or a de facto CFO. As this book of work is inevitably cyclical, being linked to the calendar year and/or based on the demands thrown at it externally by the market or internally by strategic or operational change, the COO might, at any given point of the year, wear a hat that could equally be worn by a CAO, CRO, CFO, and so on.

> *"It is inevitable that the COO role and mandate will further evolve and change, and as it does the profile of those that aspire to hold its crown will change simultaneously."*
>
> GLOBAL HEAD OF FRONT-OFFICE HUMAN RESOURCES, INVESTMENT BANKING, NEW YORK

The point here is that the role of the COO is dynamic and subject to change. This change can be driven by the industry, by regional differences, by executive personalities or by merger. The influences are numerous. One thing is for sure – the type of person who pursues this career path and the type of person that banks hire must be adaptable to survive. The requirements of the industry are changing at an unprecedented rate, so the people charged with leading it must be flexible.

Alignment: integrated or non-integrated; centralised or non-centralised

Almost without exception, the main wholesale banks (with a markets focus) started this process of change by centralising the business management function. Some banks already had this operating model in place, but governance models within these institutions habitually demonstrated inconsistencies by product and region and struggled to maximise the efficiency of such a configuration. This was perhaps compounded by the banking industry favouring the 'healthy tension' inherent in matrix management structures. In some cases, where a matrix structure existed, this led to misinterpretation of or non-compliance with the spirit of the operating model and to a lack of cohesion.

These early models, however, did establish a pre-regulatory-era precedent and demonstrated (and to a large part validated) the model and potential benefits that could be realised by such an organisational shift. The appointment of a global COO for markets was a natural conclusion to the implementation of this management model.

On the other hand, where banks had a non-integrated and/or decentralised business management function, with the business owning this headcount, some banks had (and still have) no appointed executive COO for global markets with a clear mandate of authority. In this model, the global markets' COO struggles to secure support, as no definable or obvious mandate of tenure exists in a decentralised alignment. In addition, this came about in an era when front-office COOs still sought support for their role across the bank, an understanding of their value and justification for weighty compensation. In limited examples where such an appointment did exist, it was one of influence – ambassadorial in nature, rather than possessing a quantifiable, accountable and justifiable mandate.

As this debate progressed, embedded COOs fought against the change, believing that the centralisation of the business management function would dilute their independent mandate, reduce their influence and almost certainly lead to a reduction of their compensation. COOs have expressed such concerns in the following ways:

> *"Where I would have enjoyed autonomy, working directly to and at the beck and call of my business head, I would now report up into business management function, ultimately to an executive COO of product (global COO fixed*

income or equities) or region (markets' COO Americas, Europe, MENA or Asia) or division (markets). This change, I would argue, restricts my movement and ability to make decisions quickly. This alignment would thwart the effort to move the agenda forward unheeded for business units."

MD EMEA COO, CREDIT PRODUCTS SALES AND TRADING, LONDON

"I believe strongly that to be wholly directed and owned by the business allows the COO to dedicate 100 per cent of their time to their business effort and tasks. Becoming part of a separate and centralised function, where you would service and support the business, you would invariably direct an increasing amount of your time to tasks that were cross-product or division-wide."

DIRECTOR, COO RATES TRADING, NEW YORK

"There is a perception, a deep-rooted concern, that individual compensation, and especially the variable component, is better managed when allocated directly from the business, as opposed to a centralised bonus pool for the business management function as a whole.

In the decentralised model, the COO's pay is linked to the performance of the business line they support, where the only person that has an informed insight into the value their COO adds is the business head themselves."

MD, GLOBAL COO FX, LONDON

One issue that has arisen over time is a lack of career mobility for COOs. Many rely on the patronage of their business sponsor and are vulnerable if this sponsor changes role, whether internally or externally. It is not unusual in the few banks that retain a decentralised model to find COOs who have been in the same seat for many years and/or whose careers have mirrored the progress of their patron (their business head) as they have successfully navigated their careers upwards, often taking their reliable COO with them. This could be seen as riding the coat-tails of success or conversely as an effective partnership that has realised success.

What is missing when viewing COO career advancement through this lens is the important consideration of the depth and seniority of the COO team and how this can enhance or limit career opportunities. For example, a team consisting of a few graduates and an even distribution of headcount through to managing director would create opportunities for career management, promotion and mobility over time. Alternatively, a team weighted towards experience (vice president through to managing director), which marries to the body of work better, poses career and promotional challenges. The latter model leads many to wonder where they might go next, as they wait for opportunities to unfold above them within an ageing and shrinking market.

A corporate view – one increasingly recognised by executive

management and guided by in-business human resource partners – is that this lack of mobility is not good for the individual. In particular, it limits career opportunities for junior business managers, who end up being blocked from promotion by a glass ceiling of established management. Indeed, even if these stalwart and embedded cornerstones of their respective businesses wanted to move externally, many would find it difficult, as longevity of service and experience limited to one bank are not compelling offerings as far as many senior hiring managers are concerned. By the same token, thwarting the in-business promotion of emerging talent, especially those who have received significant investment in their development by their employer, risks this asset defecting to competitors who are looking for well-practised business managers. Additionally, as control and risk are now resident at the top of the corporate agenda, relying on one person who knows the business inside and out – who has become part of its DNA – carries risks and well as benefits.

An understanding of these factors and an appreciation of the benefits that can be realised from integrating the business-management function, have led the majority of the market to move towards a fully integrated and centralised function, delivering many advantages:

- The necessity of meeting the demands of the control and conduct agenda is better served when this agenda can be expedited through a business management function that is ultimately owned by one executive manager, backed by a board mandate to drive this effort. This has invariably seen the appointment of a markets' or division-wide control officer, charged with defining the operating model for the division and then working with the principal COOs (global COO of fixed income or equities) to implement this strategy. Organisationally speaking, the control officer is a peer and, almost without exception, previously a COO and/or business head, bringing appropriate knowledge and experience to this appointment. A debate continues as to whether the control officer should sit alongside the COO at all levels in a position of equality and independence or whether the control officer should report to the COO. Currently the latter prevails; the global markets' COO retains responsibility for the control and conduct agenda, while the business heads have accountability for control itself.

2 The business management budget and associated costs are better managed when centralised, enabling the total loaded cost to be attributed, managed and quantified. Centralisation also enables cost efficiencies to be realised as, for example, transformation and change resources have greater visibility and can be allocated more efficiently to project demands division-wide.

3 Compensation structures can also be introduced division-wide, enabling both internal benchmarking (against other COOs as well as senior infrastructure management roles) and external market comparisons. This depends heavily on the collaboration of senior management, enabling calibration of compensation across functional titles, regardless of reporting lines or degree of centralisation. It also allows the bank to reward business managers in line with their individual performance, weighted against their COO peers, as opposed to the performance of the business line. A consequence of this is the ability to move business managers more easily from one product to another without facing the issue of disparate and inconsistent rewards. It does not necessarily manifest itself as a reduction in reward (see below), but puts in place a framework in which the business can manage this sizeable team more effectively.

4 Career mobility is enhanced in the centralised model, which views business management as the principal skill-set and is product agnostic. The bank can create a function that has breadth and depth and reduces reliance on the individual, while simultaneously enhancing the individual's commoditised value by diversifying that person's experience. Some see this as a sliding scale: junior COOs typically work on asset class-specific issues regardless of structure; senior COOs learn the sub-product of an asset class and are expected to apply principles broadly when designing solutions.

What has come out of this organisational shift and the impact of regulatory change is a review of the role and its desired influence and mandate. The profile of the person that occupies the role of COO is changing in line with this evolutionary process. What a bank wants its COO community to do, and what the individual is mandated and accountable for, will now define the competencies of the COO. However, while most banks retain the title 'COO', an investigation of COO responsibilities and position in each bank reveals that two mandates are now in place, and many COOs are in reality operating as CAOs.

The Chief Administration Officer

The CAO is an appointment focused on supporting and facilitating the business internally (see below), and managing the front to back and the control agenda are now the principal tasks of the CAO. There is an industry push to ensure that all reporting – previously resident on the business manager's task list – is issued by the infrastructure most logically accountable for it: finance for capital-balance sheet, P&L data, etc.; HR for headcount; and so on. In reality the business manager will get these functions to deliver information and then validate its quality with intimate knowledge of the failings of each function.

The COO needs to walk a fine line between facing off to the infrastructure functions and owning and driving them. This is where the role falls between the COO and the CAO. Many COOs believe that the shortcomings of the infrastructure distract them from their main effort, but they must be careful not 'to shoot the messenger'. For example, finance may seem incapable of performing a computation properly (system limitation/time frame, etc.), but the COO cannot always take up the slack or seek to remedy the issue in a structural manner. Many business managers find this the hardest part of their job – influencing the infrastructure function to improve itself. COOs must demand, influence and be accountable for this improvement, but they cannot execute it. They must also seek to continuously identify the next value-added element in need of improvement.

One consequence of the heavy hand of the regulator is to homogenise how divisions and businesses are run and to implement a closer relationship between COOs and their infrastructure partners. To explain this in the concrete rather than the abstract, the same reporting on approximately the same data is being produced in all the G20 banks. Over time, the emphasis on conduct topics grew, while previously EU banks had placed greater emphasis on RWA (American banks needed to catch up on RWA topics due to the reluctance of their regulator to fully implement Basel 3). This shift demands a greater level of cooperation front to back, as the cost and accountability challenges are increasingly aligned to the business's activity within its full cycle, not just the point of sale or trade. Where does this standardisation leave responsibilities in the context of the CAO?

- They are required to deliver cost reductions of a magnitude

never seen before. If such volatility in markets remains, this will be important for large platforms and vital for smaller ones, where the cost of a ticket to print is marginally higher.
- They must drive the infrastructure on behalf of the business head. This is creating a Hegelian master-slave dialectic, as the head of the business is accountable to regulators and shareholders but cannot afford to spend time on all topics and drive risk and revenues.
- There is a need to harness the infrastructure to create relevant client/market intelligence to help drive risk-adjusted revenue.

> *"The industry's CEOs and business heads own this evolutionary phase of individual company and industry-wide change, but their COOs own its execution and share its accountability. To be successful they must possess the qualities essential to promote a positive image, to be committed and passionate, energetic with an engaging manner and a strong communicator with executive presence."*
>
> MD, GLOBAL COO EQUITIES, LONDON

The Chief Operating Officer

Historically, many companies outside the financial services industry operated without a COO. Before the credit crunch began in 2007, more than 60 per cent of Fortune 500 companies did not have a COO. Since the global recession, however, this percentage has dropped significantly, as companies both within and beyond financial services began to see the advantage of having executive succession planning and shared accountability in place (to and with the CEO), as well as having top-tier executive leadership overseeing all operations. In such cases, the COO wears the mantle of a de facto CEO and must thus be of an appropriate calibre – above that of the traditional operational COO. Their competency enables the CEO to focus more fully on business strategy and the increasing burden of internal and external ambassadorial responsibilities. This mantle of being the CEO-in-waiting may be relevant outside banking, but it is not within it; there COOs are not appointed based on their potential to become the CEO but on their ability to manage the complex matters at hand within an increasingly regulated and demanding sector (see 'The Banking COO vs the non-banking COO', p. 113).

With the recession and the consequent demands by shareholders for enhanced control and risk management, banking is not the only industry to experience a resurgence in the number of COOs (although within banking this evolution is wedded to what many call the 'regulatory era'). There are good reasons, therefore, to anticipate an increased utilisation of the COO position in the future, moving its role from that of COO in title but CAO in reality to becoming an empowered partner of the CEO – a deputy CEO in all but name, with an executive mandate. The reasons for this are as follows:

- Generally, companies are becoming more global, larger and more complex, making it difficult for one person alone to have total oversight over the whole organisation.
- Companies are finding a strong relationship between strong performance and the presence of an executive COO charged with driving the business, not just supporting it.
- Companies are becoming more deliberate about CEO

succession planning and could feasibly and justifiably use the COO role to train successors and develop rising talent to move from within the business into a COO role and back into the business as part of their executive development.

- The increase in talent mobility means that the role will probably be used more often as a retention mechanism for key executives at risk of moving to a competitor.
- Regulatory change in banking is mostly driven by regional bodies, which demand a high level of local executive ownership.

These principles are notably focused on the interaction and positioning of the CEO and the COO. Nevertheless – and uniquely within banking, where the COO title is awarded across many levels, regions and products – the spirit of these conclusions can be applied to the relationship between any business heads and their COO, at any level. The principles of selecting COOs and defining their mandate can therefore be applied to any rank, from local product COO or business manager at VP level, through to a regional COO at director to managing director level, or even global-level COO as a seasoned managing director.

> *"The relationship between the Chief Executive Officer and the Chief Operating Officer in any (global non-banking) organisation is fraught with many psychological complexities. Perhaps it is the most difficult of all organisational working relationships because, more than others, it is a balancing act on the threshold of power."*
>
> HARRY LEVINSON, PSYCHOLOGIST AND CONSULTANT

However, this evolution carries risks. The interrelationship of the CEO (read 'business head') and COO is essential to the success of the business and goes hand in hand with a fully integrated and centralised operating model. To be effective, there must be a union between two strong and independent personalities who understand that they must work together in the interests of the business, its employees, clients and investors. This heightened performance and accord can only be realised where self-interest has no foothold. Within most commercial sectors, a self-effacing personality is a rare commodity, and this is perhaps even more true of the financial services industry, which has a reputation for attracting and tolerating those with a heightened opinion of their self-worth.

The selection and appointment of the COO must therefore rely strongly on an analysis of character; the COOs must marry well with the CEOs and vice versa. Between the two there must exist an understanding, a sense of respect, even an enjoyment of this partnership. Any lines of difference must be complementary, becoming lines of collaboration and not conflict. This qualitative assessment is central to the selection process. It works best when those known well to the CEO and who hold their ear can advise candidly on the selection of the COO to make this critical relationship work. In this case, CEOs may have to show sufficient humility to accept their own opinion being overridden.

Why is this relationship so important? Any breakdown in trust between the CEO and COO can lead to failure. The COO typically has to be a high-level leader who is comfortable being fully in charge. Many executives with the leadership skills necessary to be a top-level COO would prefer to run their own organisation or business line than take orders from a CEO and not directly contribute revenues. COOs who are expecting to serve their time and be promoted to a higher position may have a different timeline in mind for this movement than the CEO, causing a breakdown in the relationship. COOs can also find themselves being labelled an 'operations' person or a 'Number 2' rather than being seen as a strategic and high-level leader by the board of directors, which causes some executives to steer clear of the position.

This is especially the case in investment banking. Appointing a COO as the de facto deputy to the head of business marks a seismic shift – one that requires capital investment and an adjustment upwards in compensation. Few revenue contributors are enthusiastic about being moved into non-direct revenue-generating roles for an interim period, even if they understand that this is part of their career development and especially if short-term annual compensation is significantly and negatively impacted. The overall cost could also be a loss of revenues, as a business line loses its leader and has to adjust accordingly. However, the benefit of having a more skilled leadership team should make up for this loss over time.

> *"You can respect a technical leader at business level that delivers revenues, but would you follow him or her, are you inspired by them? There is a clear difference in securing promotion through the traditional producer-manager model (through revenue contribution), as opposed to someone that secures promotion due to their inherent and proven leadership skills. The success of a COO in the future will rely on the traditional characteristics of leadership: impact and articulation; communication and direction;*

ambition; intellect; energy and inspiration; values; innovation; subordinate development; delegation and mobilisation, self-awareness and empathy married to strength of character and conviction."

EMEA GROUP COO, EUROPEAN WHOLESALE BANK

It is a shift that will favour the brave, as they in turn embrace the demand to change the future profile of leadership and make tomorrow's executive leaders more rounded. They are also better-equipped and possess an in-depth understanding of the business front to back, the control and conduct agenda, and cost management. And they are able to define an innovative strategy, drive the business forward and remain competitive. All of this, of course, being linked to the growing burden of intrusive reviews and regulated executive accountability.

It is inevitable that the COO role and mandate will further evolve, and as it does – where bank-to-bank variances exist – the profile of those who aspire to it will change simultaneously. Some who have never considered such a position as part of their career path, and for whom a move from revenue creation to revenue support is anathema, will face this decision in the future. There will also be those who recognise that such a move would be prudent in order to maximise the chances of long-term career success. Regulators may soon demand it, and certainly many banks are likely to encourage a select few of its future leaders to make the move. However, not all will achieve success, accomplished as they may be in generating revenues and as consummate as they may be from a technical perspective. An ability to lead, instil confidence and motivate will be a fundamental requirement for success in this significantly changed, evolving and high-profile role.

It will be significant if any executive board embraces this opportunity and recognises the COO role for what it has truly become in the modern era. Decisions about who should be appointed a COO, at all levels, and how to establish a broad and deep talent pool of well-rounded and appropriately trained and educated leaders to take the business forward in the next generation will become increasingly important. Within this context, the COO role itself will come under more intense scrutiny, and many of those currently operating as CAOs to all intents and purposes may be able to step into role as truly empowered and accountable COOs.

A braver step still would be to appoint business heads who do not come from a revenue-generating background, perhaps having come up through the business management function itself. The head of the business, after all, does not have to be the highest earner in that business; the person must simply be capable of managing it effectively to meet or exceed its annual and mid- to long-term objectives, of which the key one is total revenues. One can almost hear the 'tut tut, nonsense' dismissal of business heads at this suggestion, but what proof is there that a business head, with outstanding management and leadership skills and a technical understanding of the business, could not lead a business and its sales and trading team?

So, what is really needed to be an effective COO in the modern world – beyond the traditional qualities outlined above? Certainly an effective EQ (and PQ for that matter) is one new skill required:

> *"It's harder to abuse someone and tell them to do it or they are sacked; this works on occasion, but in order to land cultural change, it needs a different style. This is polarising the population as it's simply a harder thing to teach and do. It's a generational matter, where some will embrace*

this challenge and some will simply be unwilling or incapable of doing so."

GLOBAL COO, REGIONS

What appears to be missing within the COO community as a whole is physiological resilience. Many have only known good times, organically created their own world, had limited people to answer to and been paid handsomely. Often this was entirely fair – there were, and are, a lot of capable and driven people within this community, doing great things. However, until recently they have been penalised through a marginal reduction in compensation – in 2016, 10–20 per cent of bonus against a high starting point – as there has been no real recalibration of the function or right sizing. Evidence suggests this is beginning to change, with the centralisation and greater development of the COO role. Some are undoubtedly reflecting on the demands of the role in a more pressurised era which, in addition to the reduced financial reward and apparently limited career options, makes the COO role less attractive, or at least one for those possessing physiological resilience:

"This era of change within the industry is not for the faint-hearted. It will need robust and charismatic leaders to execute it. Charisma is needed to take the business management community, and indeed the industry as a whole, through trying times ahead. They will experience uncertainty, greater levels of accountability and, I anticipate, reduced compensation."

FORMER COO

When you add limited career opportunities within a shrinking market, it is not possible to look at the changing business management and the role of the COO within it without looking at the changing skills and personality required from leaders of the banking industry to meet the demands of the new era. In the past, the best revenue-generating individuals were often promoted to desk and business heads to encourage them to forge a career path within the company. Promotion was not always based on their managerial skills. This may change as the demands of business leadership change. COOs may succeed in a business-leading role. More likely, future business heads may have to step out of a revenue-generating role into a COO or business management role to gain the experience and skills necessary to lead and manage a business. This shift would be in line with the changing COO mandate. Undoubtedly the COO is at the forefront of this evolution and will continue on a daily basis to encompass the roles and responsibilities needed to run the business, be they linked to administration (as the CAO), financial (as the CFO), risk (as the CRO) or control (as the CCO):

> *"The industry's CEOs and business heads own the opportunity and the responsibility to deliver industry-wide change, but it is the COOs who will own its execution and share its accountability."*
>
> PARTNER, FINANCIAL SERVICES PRACTICE, MANAGEMENT CONSULTING COMPANY

One of my contacts, currently the UK COO to a major European banking franchise, added colour and direction to my analysis when summarising his thoughts (outlined below). Such insights have been invaluable in shaping my understanding of the COO role, its ambiguities and points of measurement. This summary is added postscript, as it is helps contextualise some of my findings and assumptions throughout this book:

1 The term COO is undoubtedly an anachronism; there are many of them in a banking organisation. However, so is the term managing director. So we should just accept that banks have historically accepted title-creep and move on. Terminology in this case is probably a distraction.

2 Why COOs seem to be tied to the business head and not to the role… So a new business head often, though not always, means a new COO, revealing the key characteristic as 'trust' or even perception by others that the COO knows what the business head thinks – a sort of mind-reading ability developed by COOs due to their close professional relationship with the business head. How true is this, and is this a good or bad sign for the COO?

3 Career-wise, COOs are almost never going to be business heads, as they are usually focused on navigating the jungle of systems, policies, committees and cost reports that the business head needs to represent their interests, but does not have the time to do. In that regard the COO can behave as a body double, speaking on behalf of the business head and complementing that person's focus and expertise. If the COO achieves this, then his or her compensation is justified.

4 The reality is that in banking, the support and control departments are complex and expensive and can appear opaque to the commercially minded business head. COOs are is charged with focusing their energy on cutting through that complexity, whether intended or not, and getting to the heart of the proposition. Is this process needed? Is it being run in line with industry standards/best practice? Is my business being charged a fair allocation? These are all questions the business head expects the COO to be able to pose and answer.

5 Expertise-wise, COOs have a truly enviable role. They develop interpersonal, industry, process, control, analysis and reporting skills second to none. They deal with some of the brightest people on earth, from many different backgrounds, and are expected to hold their own in discussions with experts. They see the business franchise as an object they are mandated to protect and arguably are the glue that keeps the business and the bank's support and control functions connected. If they were to choose to change direction into a specific part of the bank, they could not ask for a better vantage point from which to make that decision.

6 From a regulatory perspective, COOs are crucial. Not only will they represent the business head where needed, but they are also among the few people who offer a bird's-eye view of the shape and direction of travel of the business, as well as being able to articulate the overall effectiveness of the support and control departments.

"What is the role …
your role as a markets' COO?"

THE MARKETS' COO

Evolution and responsibility in the regulatory era

Organisational alignment

In a round table discussion, it became quickly apparent that while those present were the same in title, each role differed greatly. Organisational alignment varied from the fully integrated model – with the group COO 'owning' the markets' COO and the markets' team globally, even component parts of the infrastructure – to the fully decentralised model. Here, the markets' COO reported to the markets' CEO, but did not 'directly own' the business management function and the product COOs below them. Whatever the alignment, however, it was clear that the governance structure in place impacted cross-functional and non-product-aligned activities, such as control and change.

The table overleaf shows the alignment of the key component parts within the markets' front-office business management function at the highest level. Observations drawn from this are as follows:

- The majority of markets' COOs report directly to the markets' CEO, with no report line into a group COO. With the regional nature of regulatory change, banks are increasingly appointing regional markets' COOs (EMEA out of London, Americas out of New York, Asia out of Singapore or Hong Kong). External strategy is usually a chief strategy officer appointment into the

CEO; internal strategy is usually married to 'change' and the provision of business solutions, being a report into the markets' COO.

- To address the burden of regulatory change and the consequent implications of the control agenda (1LOD), more than half of banks have appointed a divisional control officer (Chief Control Officer, CCO). This person invariably comes from a fixed-income business management background.
- A quarter of those appointed at CCO have a dotted or full line into a group CCO and the remainder into the markets' COO.

Conduct is split between conduct risk, within risk management, and a conduct lead, sitting in the CCO's office. Very few banks have not appointed a markets' conduct lead. Increasingly, the middle-office and trade-capture functions are migrating into the front-office business management function.

There are several reasons why the COO role has struggled to fully cement itself within today's C-suite. Some companies may opt to split operations responsibilities between several executives. In others, the CEO may decide to handle operational issues directly. However, in many companies, across a range of industries and regions, changing market dynamics now offer a chance to clarify the inherent logic of the COO's role – at least for those willing to take on the challenge.

Some or even much of the above may be relevant to markets within banking, but the mandate, tasks and accountability of the COO have become far more precise, and success or failure is reflected significantly in reward. The markets' COO sits over a suite of businesses (across fixed income and equities), each with its own global and regional nuances, and each business at global and regional level also has its own COO. Not surprisingly, the challenge of being a global markets' COO overseeing many businesses under

Evolution and responsibility in the regulatory era

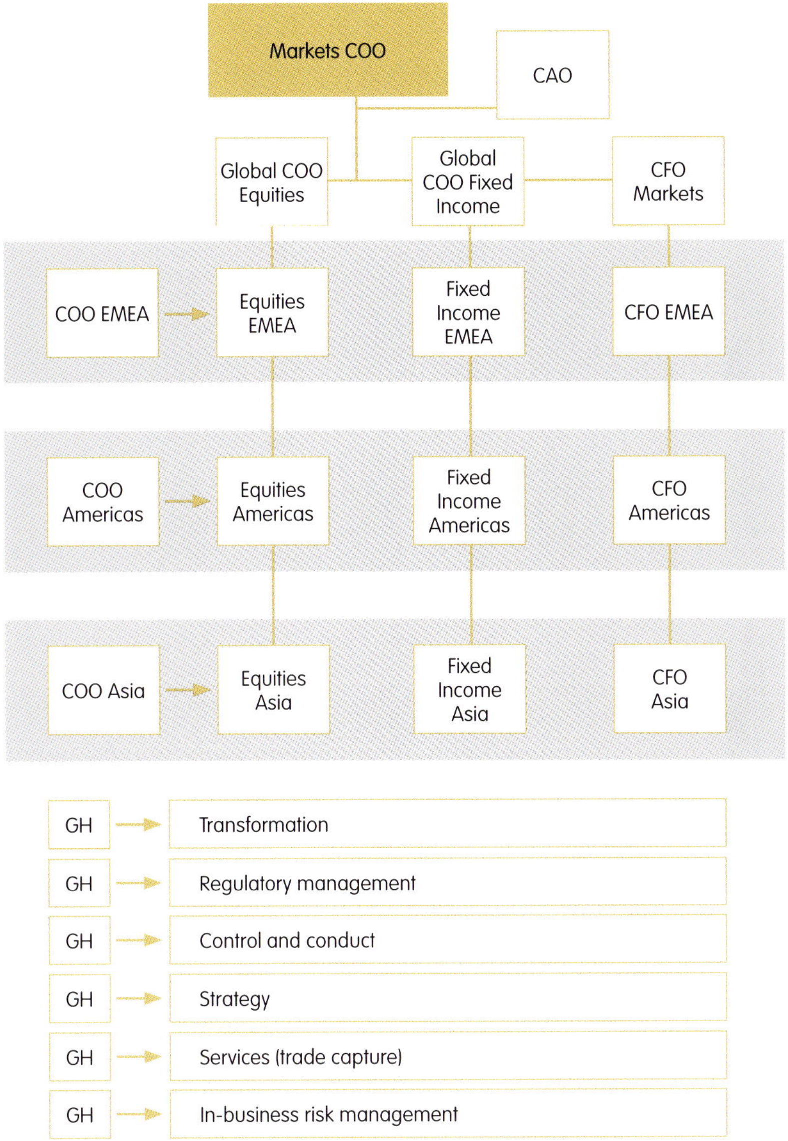

The alignment and structure of the markets division across tier 1 investment banks

	The COO markets (report into)	Centalised markets COO team (yes or no)	Regional markets COO (yes or no)	Direct report regulatory management	Front change function	
Bank 01	Group COO	COO direct ownership	No	Yes	Yes	
Bank 02	Markets' CEO	Dotted line, full line into the business (in Europe) In Asia/U.S. (COO direct ownership)	Yes	Yes	Yes	
Bank 03	Group COO	Dotted line	Yes	Yes	Yes	
Bank 04	Market CEO, Global Head of CIB ITO	Full line into the business	Yes, U.S./Asia reporting into the GM COO	No separate FO risk function	Yes	
Bank 05	Geographic COO	Into the business locally and dotted line into the regional bank COO	No	Yes	Not in region	
Bank 06	IB COO, FICC CEO (replicated in equities, i.e., no markets' COO with COO ownership)	Business-owned COO teams, FICC/IB COO-owned central team	Yes, regional FICC COOs.	Yes, business implementation	Yes	
Bank 07	Global Markets Head	Direct into business	No	No	No	
Bank 08	Capital Markets' CEO and Group CFO (dotted line)	Direct into business head, dotted line into COO/CAO	Yes, U.S., Asia and U.K. reporting into the CM COO	No	Yes	
Bank 09	Markets CEO	Yes	No	Yes	Product COOs, not central	
Bank 10	Hard line into CEO and dotted into Group COO	Yes, although strong sense of business ownership	Yes	Yes	Yes	

	Markets CFO reporting into the markets' COO? (yes or no)	Strategy (the CSO)	Conduct & control (The CCO)	Trade capture or middle office	Other	Global business management headcount (not including middle office)
	Same person	Yes	Yes	No	Conduct centralised in group	150
	No	Involved in strategy but not the leader	Yes	No		220
	No	No	Yes	No	Client lifestyle management	150
	No	No	No separate FO risk function	No	GM communication, ITO process/ organisational; large transversal/ front-to-back project	150 FO 50 CIB ITO
	No	Product strategy led globally; business strategy for region set locally, within parameters of global risk appetite	Reports to COO at group			230
	No	No	Yes	No	Large front-to-back projects; technology planning	c.160 (80 for FICC and 80 for equities)
	No	Yes	Yes for GM division	No	Business management, FO risk and control, client on boarding, client analytics, FO IT	c.90
	No	Yes	Yes for CM-wide effort	CM Ops - yes	CM ops, data management, business transformation (change management)	c.220
	No	Yes	Yes	Yes	Markets' executive COO team, very light, with macro- and micro- COOs driving the agenda	240
	Yes	Yes	Yes	No		280

one umbrella has its complexities. It is the unique ability to be charged with managing a number of COOs (some directly, some indirectly) while handling the reigns of collective accountability that sets the role apart. A markets' COO has to be adept at managing resources both directly and indirectly. This is often difficult when facing strength of character and a sense of individual purpose in a counterpart during the decision-making process.

Concentric circles of responsibility

New business dynamics redefining an old role

The following factors underscore the need for a strong leader, with operational orientation experience, especially within the increasingly complex business environment of global banking:

- A daunting regulatory environment.
- A tougher emphasis on efficiency and cost management, including a drive to transform many core aspects of the business.
- The need to seek out, validate and expand into new products and markets in the pursuit of growth.

These needs are also highlighted by the increasing speed of change, from ever-shorter product development life cycles to a continuously evolving technology. The effects of this are clearly felt by today's COOs. As Ernst & Young LLP's report, *The DNA of the COO; Resetting the logic of the COO's role* outlines:

> *"One in three of those polled says that increased complexity and a wider set of tasks have been the most striking change in their job over the past five years."*

The COO has pivotal role, sitting at the heart of many business activities

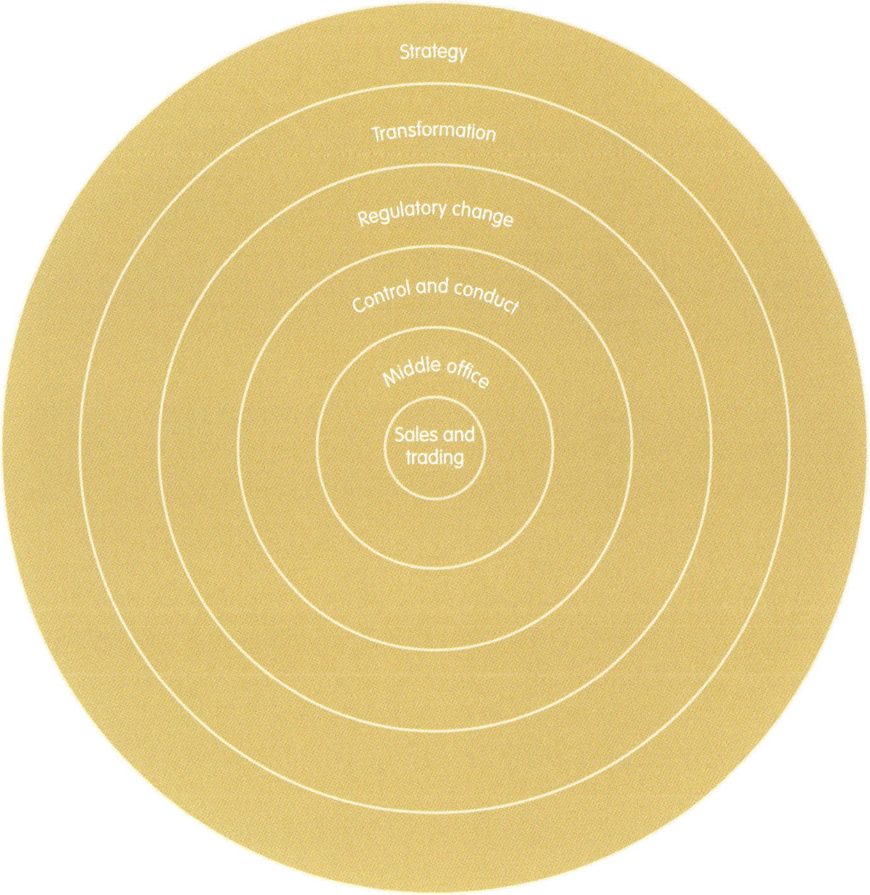

Summary of changed tasks for a COO (2010–15)

When asked, the COOs in place now, reconciling the demands of the role up to five years ago, make note of the following:

- Increasing complexity of the regulatory environment.
- Increasing pressure on efficiencies.
- Growing importance of the strategic and future operating model.
- Being up to date with technology trends.
- Increasing risk and compliance issues.
- Improving the management structure and communication from the board throughout the business, front to back.
- Growing importance of process management and standardised/best practises.
- Increased demand on demonstrating management competencies.

The common threads running through the eight points above are control and cost, but there is also accountability to deliver this control and drive change to deliver the cost savings. COOs are being asked to do more and to do better with less, in the pursuit not just of competitive advantage, but as one COO stated:

> *"... To stay operational, to stay alive, to be one of the few left standing as we try to marry falling revenues with the cost demands of implementing regulatory change".*

Change brings opportunity

It is not all bad news, as there will still be a banking sector after the regulatory era. It will be different, certainly – reshaped, likely better managed and more highly regulated – but there will be a new platform for the next generation to innovate and deliver new services and products within the confines of the new world. For ambitious COOs, all this provides a significant opportunity. More than any other executive, COOs are well placed to take on such challenges and cement their position within the organisation.

Furthermore, the CEOs of today should understand that throughout this change, they cannot successfully operate, and will not deliver on investors' and clients' expectations, without a COO of the highest calibre. Not least, the COO is there to ensure that the CEO, carrying collective responsibility for the business, remains this side of the prison bars. This fact alone has been enough for most banking CEOs and business heads to choose their right-hand man or woman very carefully. Hiring the right COO can also free up the CEO to focus on setting the corporate vision and goals, while then relying on the operational leader, the COO, to shape and implement the underlying strategy. In some banks, this also acts as a form of succession planning, as future business leaders migrate through the role of COO, shaping them into a more rounded and relevant business head.

Adapting to the environment

Unlike other management roles, such as the CFO, there are no professional standards for the COO, nor are expectations of the job common across all organisations. Rather than possessing a single set of skills that can be easily identified in any business, COOs have to adapt, chameleon-like, to the environment in which they find themselves. A common call of COOs is, 'It is up to us to prove that we're bringing added value. We need to do a better job of marketing ourselves.' COOs will greatly increase their chances of success in the role if they can demonstrate clearly to other members of the C-suite the value that they bring.

Important, but not indispensable?

In general, markets' COO C-suite peers have great respect for the demands of the role. Yet, when it comes to the question of whether a company would perform worse if it had no COO, opinions differ, especially at a level or two down in the infrastructure. The real value of an in-business COO is known only by the head of the business/the CEO or those in close proximity to the COO.

COOs need to work more at self-promotion and communication in order to raise the value-add profile of the role. This is not about self-justification, but rather an effort to foster a greater understanding of the role and influence of the COO across the bank – to the benefit of all. For the CEO, the COO is both the lubricant keeping the wheels of the business turning and the glue keeping all working parts together. This dual role is sometimes misunderstood or not understood at all.

Areas where a COO's work adds value to a company

In the same way that CEOs and business founders require entrepreneurial skills to devise new business ideas and create a culture of product and service innovation, the COO must also be entrepreneurial. Besides taking responsibility for the diverse day-to-day operational demands, COOs in many banks handle larger business-transformation initiatives and have started to drive strategy. A mastery of change management is therefore a core part of the role for many and perhaps even how the position was secured in the first place. The willingness to embrace change requires COOs to be comfortable making decisions.

In general, COOs seem to be measured on the following criteria:

- Increasing efficiency within business operations.
- Keeping to the budget and meeting investor demands.
- Realising cost savings (and realising future business benefit).
- Performance and agility of the business management and supporting operational functions.
- Leadership skills and engendering a culture of loyalty performance and innovation.
- Improving the company's financial metrics and governance.
- Improving company's ethical standing, especially in relation to control and the regulatory agenda.
- Strategic planning and the mindset of the overall leadership team.
- Ability to attract, hire, train and retain talented people.

The new go-to person for bankwide transformational initiatives

When asked, a high percentage of markets' COOs stated that they were closely engaged in discussing the role that operations and the infrastructure could play in business transformation and changing the future state of the business. A higher percentage, however, believed they should spend more time and have more input in helping to structure wholesale change within the bank, possibly moving the ownership of operations and technology directly under the business. This in itself is a return to the beginning of time, when the COO did indeed own everything behind the trade, its findings drawn from a COO forum that proposed the question, "How does the COO community reshape the conversation with operations and technology?"

Talent management

The COO has the chance to take responsibility for an initiative, which could turn it from being a decision based upon a wholly operational perspective to a more strategic one. It also offers the opportunity for the markets' COO fraternity to cooperate to change the state of banking in ways that previous market-wide efforts (Swift, CLS, Swapwire and others) have not allowed.

In such a hypothetical position, the COO would control the allocation and prioritisation of corporate resources and assets to achieve the strategic goals. Once a decision has been made, the COO must ensure that the right resources are in the right places. There is thus a strong link between this aspect of the role and people development. As with all aspects of their role – past, present and increasingly the future – COOs must be deeply involved in talent management.

Joining the strategic inner circle

COOs may need not only to master operational excellence, but also to become a driver of strategy. This switch in focus highlights a dichotomy in the role of the COO today. On the one hand, COOs must focus their attention on the here and now. This demands a deep involvement in operations to ensure that they are performing at optimal level company-wide. On the other hand, they must find the space to shape longer-term strategy, because they are best placed to assess the extent to which they actively engage with the board on key issues:

- Discussing business performance and decision-making.
- Driving operational innovation by embracing technologies.
- Driving operational transformation and direction front to back.
- Realising operational efficiencies and standardisation.

Thriving on challenges, rising above complexity, here now the markets' COO

The main challenge for COOs is carving out the space to showcase their skills. It requires them to find a ladder out of the operational trenches, to gain a wider perspective of the business. But such challenges are what COOs thrive on. When asked what makes their role worthwhile, respondents point to the fact that it brings fresh challenges every day. They also enjoy engaging with a wide variety of different functions and departments across the business.

Markets' COOs need to challenge the common perception that the role is primarily concerned with keeping the wheels turning and little else, dealing with and executing the regulatory agenda, meeting the demands of the business from day to day. To overcome this, they must demonstrate that they make a strategic contribution to the business and that their role 'moves the needle' on business performance. They must show they can, if required, run the business, regardless of the fact that many of them lack experience in managing risk.

Some say that COOs need to capitalise on their unique vantage point and now is the time to do this. How? By getting involved in almost every function, COOs can spot interdependencies and help integrate activities across the business. They can break down functional and geographical silos and identify ways of combining assets to drive efficiencies and transfer best practise.

The markets' COO may carry different responsibilities bank to bank, and the weighting of these responsibilities may vary, but they do carry the heavy burden of collectively shaping key component parts of the banking industry. This can be achieved by working with internal leadership as well as with peers industry-wide.

THE COO V CAO

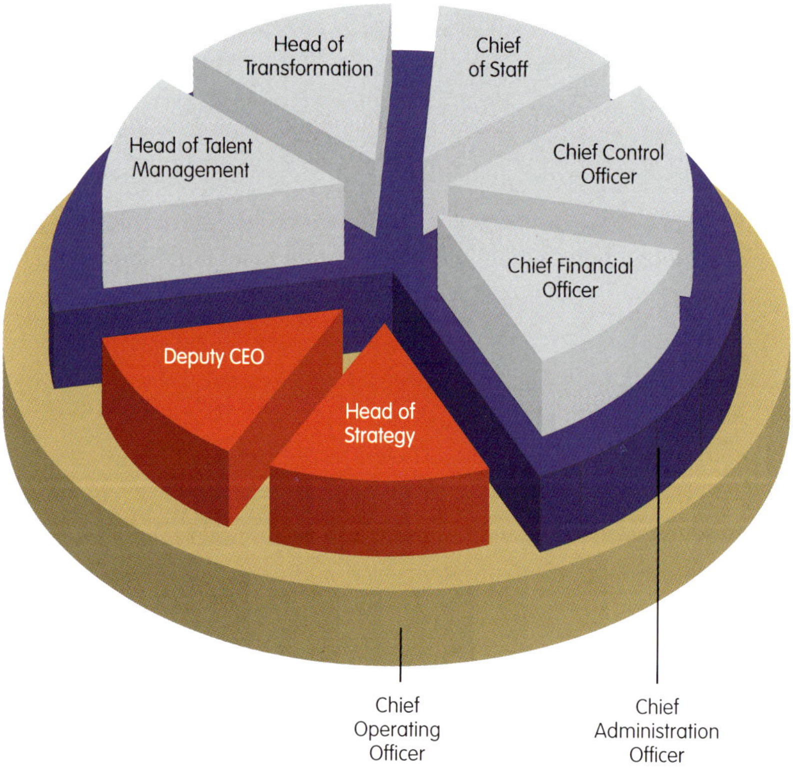

"It would be difficult to classify my role in one of the seven boxes. It was an amalgamation of all those roles. As COO, my responsibilities were to run a successful business and to help the CEO of the business achieve his or her goals. On occasion, successful traders or salespeople were thrust onto management roles with no real business experience. This would be similar to asking a baseball player to run Major League Baseball after a successful season hitting or pitching. In these situations, a COO would need to guide a head trader or salesperson on how to run a business. Sometimes the new head would have no interest in learning the details of the business and would implicitly have the COO to run the day to day".

FORMER GLOBAL COO, INSTITUTIONAL SALES

"The challenge when making any organisational changes is convincing business heads that it is not taking away their right-hand man/woman, restricting the bespoke nature of this key supporting asset, but is rather making this role more effective for both the business heads and the business as a whole."

NEW HORIZONS AND TROUBLED WATERS

A quantification of value

New horizons and a higher threshold for performance frames the future of business management, as CEOs seek quantification of value and COOs feel the squeeze of accountability.

CEOs drive organisational change

Increasing regulatory demands, cost containment/management, a focus on maintaining and sustaining profitability while seeking growth through hard work and innovation, all within a distressed market where every bank is struggling to maintain market share within a shrinking market … these are the embedded dynamics being managed by today's leaders of the banking industry. When such pressures are combined with the challenges of securing and retaining the best people to deliver success, today's CEOs and business heads claim commercial leadership is far more difficult and diverse than in the past. In addition, the levels of regulated accountability for this leadership are distinct and far from those that went before them:

> *"Business leadership in 2016 is somewhat a distant cousin to that of pre-2008. To achieve my objectives I need a different tool kit, different*

people possessing a different mentality. One of the cornerstones of successful executive management in banking, in my opinion, is in defining the role of the COO (front office) in the modern context, then selecting the right person to undertake this role (and not compromising in this selection) and working with my COO to make him or her effective. My COO and I must make one, my shortcomings made good by his or hers. In making the right decision, in ensuring the role is defined, this will make me more productive, enhance my performance, ability to focus on revenues and strategy and, most importantly, business delivery".

This summarised quote from a leading investment banker represents a very modern interpretation of the role and importance of the COO (for which, read business manager, chief of staff, front-office CAO). It somewhat counters the traditional view of the 'business manager', who, in some cases:

"… appears to spend the majority of his or her time duplicating the work already undertaken by other departments for no other reason than to ensure the well-constructed and detailed reports delivered from elsewhere are actually reliable".

This role appears to have evolved in part because of the mistrust that can exist between departments (specifically the business and some of its support functions) and their consequent inability to work effectively together. However, our research clearly demonstrates that what historically has been a 'nice to have' has now become a role of great impact, influence and necessity. This is particularly true in an era when COOs increasingly find themselves at the heart of the regulatory agenda.

In some cases, company-dependent quantification of value is now being sought for the business management function, bringing the value of individual COOs under equal scrutiny:

> *"My global COO function in reward alone cost me somewhere in the region of £50 million in 2015 – this before any control allocated headcount is taken into account. It is my responsibility to understand how this investment is being spent, what the function does and to ensure that the firm gets £50 million of value from this investment. We are some way from this point, but uniformity, transparency and consistency in mandate and indeed reward will enable me to do this more effectively".*
>
> HEAD OF PRODUCT CONTROL, GLOBAL INVESTMENT BANK

The challenge when making any organisational changes is convincing business heads that it is not taking away their right-hand man/woman, restricting the bespoke nature of this key supporting asset, but is rather making this role more effective for both the business heads and the business as a whole.

The role, its mandate and its perception vary significantly

from bank to bank and, in many companies, from one business line to another. There now exists a market-wide recognition that a different level of executive is needed in these roles today, which brings a requirement to hire upper-quartile talent into these roles and to carry the cost associated with rising reward for key players within the COO market. This in itself shines a spotlight on the role and the broader business management function.

Talent does not come cheap in a sector where the pool is relatively small and where those who have successfully adjusted to the increasing demands on the COO (be they regulatory, control or risk responsibilities) are even more rare. There is a significant difference between a 'run-the-business' COO – at any level – and one who has a proven track record of driving change to help business growth and/or performance. Importantly, while the core behavioural and technical competencies may be defined, a suitable personality fit with the business head is essential. When this qualitative component comes into play, selection and retention of the best COOs can be very difficult.

Market dynamics and the challenge for the COO can therefore be summarised as follows:

- Continued pressures across the industry and evolving demands on business heads have manifested themselves in a change within the accountability, visibility and demands on the business management function.
- This dynamic function is having to respond quickly to the change and while many would argue that they are being paid less for doing more and carrying increased accountability, the upside is that the role is now more valued (and perhaps understood) and varied than ever before.

Key areas of common and market-wide consideration – and what is resident in the COO's in-tray – are outlined below, along with historic reward and compensation. The latter, however, has significant variables, and even the best analysis is not wholly reliable due to the differences from bank to bank and role to role.

Key dynamics within the COO community

1 Review of the organisational design of the business management function with, for example, a number of banks having moved some operational components into front office (e.g., trade capture), with many banks at group level also citing headcount growth within the business management function as a growing concern and in need of review and validation.

2 The feasibility of the merger of the COO and business management functions at group and divisional level (at divisional level, for example within IB/markets, the integration of sales and trading within business management).

3 Organisational review of the 1LOD programme and allocation of headcount to the control and conduct effort and the interrelationship and ownership of tasks with operational Risk/2LOD.

4 How is change managed? The centralised approaches are being scrutinised at many banks, with an additional focus on the development of low-cost centres, on- or offshore for front-office headcount.

5 Dealing with industry-wide change and, in particular, the impact on fixed-income markets and how all banks, to one degree or another, are restructuring their fixed-income divisions.

6 Title review, with many in the market understanding that the title of COO has been diluted and lost its equity and brand value in recent years, recognising that many (or even most) COOs are in fact by task a CAO or business manager. Some banks have already removed the title of COO in many instances to reinforce the mandate and seniority of the COO title itself.

7 Compensation and reward annual review with an adjustment and compensation compression in quarter one 2016.

Compensation for the COO community: 2014–2017 and the inevitability of falling reward

The difficulty of securing reliable compensation data within front-office business management is well understood. However, as the 2016 bonus announcements were pending or in the final stages of dissection and allocation, we anticipated compensation across the COO market to be equal at best (and would be down for many at senior director and managing director levels).

In a market segment where no single position matches another, and where the demands on the business management function are increasing and possess greater impact and accountability, getting the reward right is of course fundamental. A bank does not need to be number one in the 'pay league', but it does needs to be in sight of the podium to retain the best people. The question for all banks, therefore, is whether the compensation carried forward every year remains competitive. Where relevant, banks need to ask how much weight they should give to counter-organisational dynamics, with many banks still dealing with unsettling periods. This will continue to influence the level of interest people have in looking externally. Many believed the 2016 bonus round would be important in defining the parameters of reward for years to come. It will be interesting to see if there is common ground market-wide in the future.

Looking at the compensation tables (pages 108 and 109), it is easier to get reasonably accurate data at bands 4 and 5 (vice president and director), but it remains a challenge to benchmark managing director bands 1 to 3 accurately. Within this analysis, MD band 1 would be an IB/market COO/divisional board-level appointment.

It is worth reiterating the key point about business management being a discipline, and its reward is that it has the greatest disparity in compensation across the banking sector, including some significant outliers at director and managing director level. These exceptions can be paid well above the upper quartile (which have been discounted within our analysis). These outliers are usually found within banks where the business management function and/or the product COOs are paid directly from the business rather than from a centralised bonus pool or structured framework for compensation. Sometimes the appointee has been moved from a revenue-generating role as part of her or his career development.

The market can make some significant savings by bringing in a level of uniformity across its IB/markets' COO function (and braver banks looking further into group, as the potential 'owner' of the COO function across all divisions) in relation to reward. A more centralised approach on compensation and more specifically issuance/ownership of the bonus pool by the IB/markets' COO, as opposed to the business or other, would facilitate this process and benefit. This is the model that can be found in almost all principal banks today.

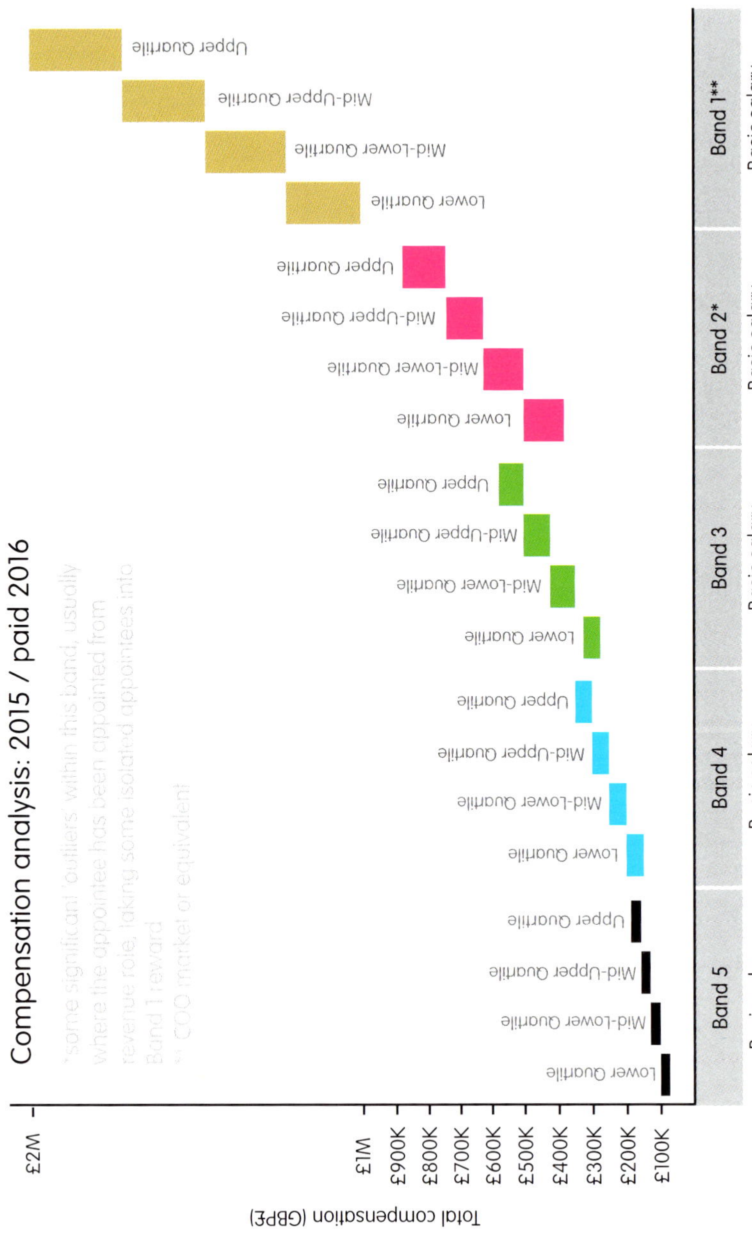
Compensation analysis: 2015 / paid 2016
*some significant 'outliers' within this band, usually where the appointee has been appointed from revenue role, taking some isolated appointees into Band 1 reward
** COO market or equivalent
Total compensation (GBP£)
£2M
£1M
£900K
£800K
£700K
£600K
£500K
£400K
£300K
£200K
£100K
Lower Quartile
Mid-Lower Quartile
Mid-Upper Quartile
Upper Quartile
Band 5
Basic salary £70K - £125K
Band 4
Basic salary £130K - £175K
Band 3
Basic salary £250K+
Band 2*
Basic salary £250K+
Band 1**
Basic salary £250K+

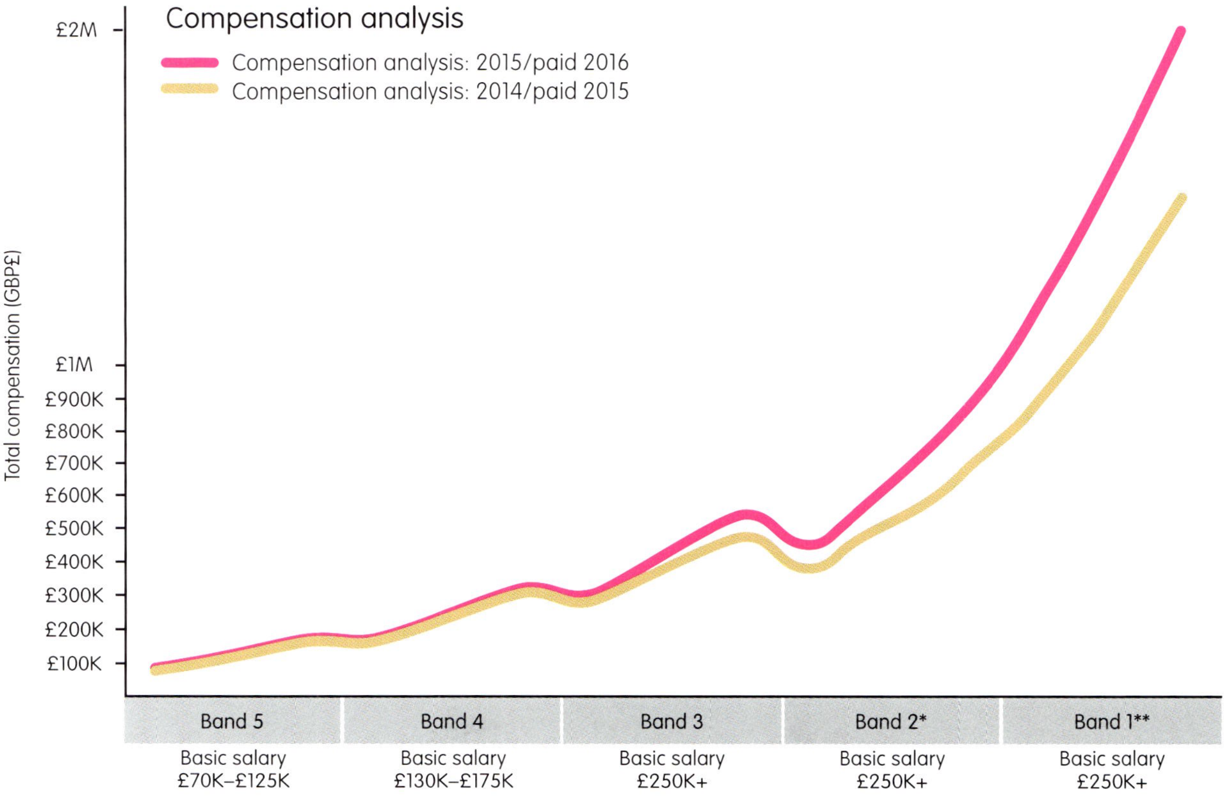
Compensation analysis
Compensation analysis: 2015/paid 2016
Compensation analysis: 2014/paid 2015
Total compensation (GBP£)
£2M
£1M
£900K
£800K
£700K
£600K
£500K
£400K
£300K
£200K
£100K
Band 5
Basic salary £70K–£125K
Band 4
Basic salary £130K–£175K
Band 3
Basic salary £250K+
Band 2*
Basic salary £250K+
Band 1**
Basic salary £250K+

"Trust lies at the heart of any COO-CEO relationship. The bridge of confidence between two people operating together with separate yet united agendas is essential for this relationship to work."

THE BANKING COO v NON-BANKING COO

Non-identical twins

The roles have a common name and common behavioural traits, but there ends their commonality. The limited reading material available on the role of the COO focuses almost exclusively on the COO within commerce and industry. While there are fleeting references to the banking industry within these papers and books, it is on the execution of the COO role in well-known (and usually global) non-banking corporates that each centres its attention.

For our purposes – looking at the world through a financial services lens – this focus is certainly worthy of consideration, as it helps frame the discussion on the banking COO. It also helps demonstrate the uniqueness and the peculiarity of the role within the financial markets.

Outside the banking sector, the COO is appointed as the CEO-in-waiting. The selection process is primed to provide someone possessing the experience required to replace the CEO in time. This is not relevant for all non-banking companies and large corporates, but it is a central and common point in most of the papers, articles and books analysing COOs and their mandate.

At the time of writing this article, there is a trend towards migration of some business or product heads into a COO role within banking. Such movements from a direct revenue role into a non-revenue contribution role are limited, but as compensation has merged between the two (trading or sales and executive business management or COO roles), and the need to understand regulation, governance and control as a business head is now a prerequisite, this previously unthought-of career choice has become more acceptable to revenue creators. The change is driven by the evolving landscape of banking and the dawn of the new regulatory era. Banking business leaders must now possess an understanding of their business front to back and the implications of the regulatory agenda.

Indeed, under such regulations as the Senior Managers Regime, banking heads and their executive management teams in the U.K. have become accountable for their departments to an unprecedented level. When someone holds collective responsibility for all aspects of the business, the way in which they look at internal matters will undoubtedly be far sharper than ever before, as is the regulation's design. Today it is to the COO that the CEO and/or business heads (whenever we note CEO here, we include business heads) turn for assurance about the control framework and its effectiveness in preventing or identifying potential breaches that could have significant corporate and personal consequences.

Into this space steps the reshaped role of the banking COO, and into this role step tomorrow's business leaders. The COO role has become a medium for career advancement in the modern era; those passing through it emerge equipped to be the future business heads and CEOs. Through the COO experience they are better prepared, more rounded and capable of handling the complex and diverse responsibilities of the CEO in today's highly regulated and controlled banking sector.

The dissection of the COO role outside banking can help us understand the evolving role of the COO within it. The following is an analysis of one of the more recognised papers (from

Nathan Bennett and Stephen A. Miles' *Second in Command; the misunderstood role of the Chief Operating Officer*, reprinted by permission of Harvard Business Review, Vol. 84, No. 5, 2006) investigating the role of the COO. In going over the key points raised and examining their relevance (or not) to the banking COO, we can reconcile areas of commonality and pinpoint areas of difference.

Second in Command – the misunderstood role of the Chief Operating Officer

When Larry Ellison, founder and CEO of Oracle, and his chief operating officer, Ray Lane, parted ways in 2000, the event inspired the kind of breathless reporting usually reserved for celebrity divorces. Forbes.com reporter David Einstein wondered in print, 'Did Lane quit or was he fired?' and wished he had 'a clue as to why Ellison's second banana for the past eight years suddenly was cleaning out his office.' Soon afterwards, CNET News.com weighed in with this: 'The story of Lane's plight at one of the most powerful companies in technology is one of hubris, greed, betrayal and personal epiphany…' Readers were left with two puzzles to sort out. First: Why Lane was leaving his position, given what seemed to be an unbroken string of admirable achievements. And second: Why the event was wrapped in such drama. Executives change posts all the time, yet the story, with its hints of palace intrigue and titanic clashes, was inherently captivating.

For us, it was another example suggesting that the role of the COO is, well, different. Our research since then has put a finer point on the difference. Through in-depth conversations with dozens of executives who have held the position and with CEOs who have worked with COOs, we've gained insight into a subject that has been largely neglected by organizational scholars. Our discoveries shed light not only on the dramatic executive breakups that intermittently make headlines but also on the successful experiences of many unsung COOs. In this article, we share the success and failure factors we've identified, as well as our analysis of such related questions as: Are there circumstances in which a number two role is particularly useful? Are there situations when it will inevitably produce tension and discord?

Understanding what makes for a successful chief operating officer is vital because the effectiveness of COOs (or ranking operations executives by whatever name they are called) is critical to the fortunes of many companies—and could be to many more. As we will suggest, the second-in-command executive is a role that by rights should become increasingly prevalent. It is prevented from doing so, perhaps, because it is so misunderstood.

It was rumoured that Ray Lane became the sacrificial lamb after a dubious investigation by Oracle into Microsoft (by Oracle) led to Lane's sudden exit. Some have argued that Larry Ellison enjoyed the limelight, and while Lane had similar ambitions, the two men were never going to form a successful partnership (see Forbes 7/5/2000). It is difficult for two strong personalities to share authority effectively, and although there are exceptions, it often becomes a case of 'two is a crowd'. The implications for a business can be significant – in the worst cases leading to a fracture within it as two or more leaders divide to conquer.

The above is supposition, but it raises important questions about the mandate, power base, career platform and prospects of the COO. In banking, the COO is not (or very rarely) appointed as the CEO-in-waiting, but is rather someone whose skill-set and experiences complement those of the CEO. The COO's priority is to relieve the CEO of the burden of internal management, regulation, change and so on. This allows the CEO to focus his or her efforts on strategy, investor relationships, revenue creation and any aspects that directly impact the business's ability to secure or retain clients, develop new products, create revenue and drive the business forward. The

COO partners this effort by ensuring the business is compliant, controlled, and efficient. The COO will seek ways to drive down costs and deliver value to the bottom line, while the CEO focuses on the top line. Today, this contribution to shareholder value is no less important.

A unique point of reference

When you start to examine COOs as a class, one thing immediately becomes clear: There are almost no constants. People with very different backgrounds ascend to the role and succeed in it. This variability makes the job difficult to study; it's hard to know whether you are making proper inferences when comparing one COO with another.

Salespeople or marketers who have developed the tools of their trade in one company can usually apply them to good advantage in another, even in a dramatically different industry. Financial and human resource executives likewise are schooled and practiced in standard ways of doing things. But it's hard to discern whether a COO who has succeeded in one company has what it takes to be COO in another; the skill-set is neither generic nor very portable. Even within a single company, the right qualifications for the COO role can shift. Maynard Webb, COO at eBay, described for us the difference between his own technology background and that of his predecessor: 'The first COO, Brian Swette, had a job that was nothing like my job....Brian was a sales and marketing guy. He had the business units reporting directly to him and spent no time on any of my role.'

It's difficult to pinpoint the kinds of environments in which COOs thrive. While there is a general sense that COOs are most prevalent in operations-intensive businesses, they appear in every kind of company, and every sector also features firms without them. Moreover, the same organization may sometimes operate with a COO and sometimes without one. A 2003 study by Crist Associates, for example, showed that only 17% of the corporations that promoted a COO to CEO in the previous year had replaced the COO.

Finally, there is no single agreed-upon description of what the job entails or even what it's called. Often, companies turn responsibility for all areas of operations over to the COO—this typically includes production, marketing and sales, and research and development. In some firms, the job is to be Mr. Inside to the CEO's Mr. Outside. In others, the mission is focused on a specific business need. For example, last summer Microsoft filled the long-vacant position of COO with Kevin Turner from Wal-Mart. In announcing his appointment, the company stated that Turner was expected to use his retail experience to lead Microsoft's effort to grow the consumer products business. The most cursory survey of COO job designs shows real disparity in spans of control, decision rights, reporting structures, and the like.

It is correct to state the "the right qualifications for the COO role can shift", as this has been a necessity within banking, as much of a COO's time is now dedicated to driving change. This change agenda is defined by cost and regulation, and the role of the COO has become more inward-looking as a result.

Unlike the sentiment outlined above, generally a banking COO is not hired to build a new business or to strategically take the business on a new journey, but rather to execute the vision and strategy of the CEO and his or her principal business leaders. This is consistent, as is a deep-rooted commonality in purpose and tasks from one banking COO to another, particularly within markets. The common challenges of falling revenues, cost-ratio implications and the burden of the regulatory agenda create a single purpose. This is the reason for Armstrong Wolfe's success in getting a COO peer group around a table on a quarterly basis since 2014 to discuss common market-wide challenges. While there exists at its core shared aims and challenges, the broader parameters of responsibility and influence can vary greatly from bank to bank, reconciling with the idea that the "most cursory survey of COO job designs shows real disparity in spans of control, decision rights, reporting structures, and the like".

How can a title accommodate such diversity and still be meaningful? Answering that question requires a shift in perspective. The key is in the orientation of the role. While other jobs are primarily defined in relation to the work to be done and the structure of the organization, the COO's role is defined in relation to the CEO as an individual.

As we will explore in the following section, that relationship can take various forms. In many cases, the COO is there to help make the CEO's vision a reality. Sometimes, the COO is expected to make the CEO more effective or more complete. Often, the plan is for the COO ultimately to fill the CEO's shoes. But in all of these constructions, the CEO is the magnetic force with which the COO must align. This makes asking the question 'What makes a great COO?' akin to asking, 'What makes a great candidate for U.S. vice president?' A Southern Baptist? A foreign-policy wonk? A charismatic campaigner? A centrist? It all depends on the other half of the equation, the first name on the ticket. This, then, is why COOs remain mysterious as a class: The role is structurally, strategically, socially, and politically unique—and extraordinarily situational.

One of the challenges faced by the executive COO in banking is the dilution of the title within the sector. The key, therefore, is not just the "orientation of the role" but defining the exact authority of it, which is difficult when the title is sprinkled throughout an organisation.

Some banks have sought to address this, removing the title 'COO' from many managerial employees and replacing it with 'business manager', but even here there is still much work to be done around internal communications to ensure that the COO's mandate and authority are well understood.

Additionally, I would counter the conclusion: "While other jobs are primarily defined in relation to the work to be done and the structure of the organization, the COO's role is defined in relation to the CEO as an individual." As noted above, the COOs role in banking is largely defined by a book of work that is regulatory and cost related. This is relevant at its core, but the organisational nuances bank to bank would support the statement that the role is 'structurally, strategically, socially, and politically unique—and extraordinarily situational'.

Seven kinds of COO

If the COO role is defined primarily in relation to the CEO, and no two CEOs are exactly alike, does that mean the job simply defies definition? Not quite. What became clear in the course of our research is that the differences among COO roles arise from the different motives behind creating the position in the first place. It turns out there are seven basic reasons why companies decide to hire a COO, and these yield seven roles that COOs can play vis-à-vis their CEOs. Readers will recognize that the seven reasons are not mutually exclusive, though in this initial presentation we treat them as such.

We have touched on the principal motive for the existence, not the creation, of the banking COO, but essentially it is a fundamental building block, the foundation upon which the success of the CEO and/or the business heads is built. It is fundamental in assuring that the business operates in a controlled, compliant and increasingly cost-effective way. It is fundamental in operating as both the glue and the oil that allows the revenue generators to carry out their own roles effectively and in good order. It is fundamental in that it works well only when the partnership, the competencies and individual ambitions of the CEO and COO are aligned.

The executor

One role of a COO is to lead the execution of strategies developed by the top management team. It's simply a concession to the complexity and scope of the CEO's job today, with its numerous external commitments. Managing large, often global, enterprises sometimes requires two sets of hands; in such cases, the COO typically takes responsibility for delivering results on a day-to-day, quarter-to-quarter basis.

This is why the COO position is nearly ubiquitous in businesses that are operationally intensive, like the airline and automotive industries, as well as in organizations that operate in hypercompetitive and dynamic marketplaces like high-tech firms. At Seagate Technology, for example, CEO Bill Watkins relies on COO David Wickersham to keep the business performing at its peak. It's not that Watkins lacks an execution mindset himself; in fact, he ascended to his post after excelling as COO to the previous CEO, Stephen Luczo. But the demands of managing an $8 billion vertically integrated disk drive business are substantial. By bringing in a COO to lead and oversee the day-to-day operations, Seagate allows Watkins to focus on the strategic, longer-term challenges the company will face. CEO Watkins is clearly oriented with his 'head up' to understand success in the future, whereas COO Wickersham has his 'head down,' focused on the operational details necessary for success today.

This applies in banking to some degree, but not entirely. As we have seen, the COO is a 'pair of hands' to execute the CEO's vision. The analysis is correct in a literal sense, but not when you put this execution into context. Outside banking, COOs will take this vision and often have under them component parts of the business, such as research, marketing and sales, to carry out this strategy. They will lead the business effort, rather than supporting and facilitating it, as is the responsibility of the banking COO.

It is also important to understand what 'operations' means in the context of banking and outside it. Outside banking, 'operations' can encompass the whole institution – all departments from sales through technology to financial control. Within banking, it alludes to the support functions only. The banking COO faces inwards and downwards into 'operations', ensuring the operational platform (be it risk, finance, compliance, legal or core operations) is providing the services required for the business to operate. The COO will execute the component parts of the CEO's strategy from a banking perspective, which is somewhat different to the mandate of many COOs outside the sector.

The change agent

Just as Microsoft did when it hired Kevin Turner, some companies name a COO to lead a specific strategic imperative, such as a turnaround, a major organizational change, or a planned rapid expansion. While the mandate is not as broad as the general execution of strategy, the magnitude of the challenge demands that the change-agent COO have a degree of unquestioned authority similar to that of an executor COO. This was, in fact, what led to Ray Lane's arrival at Oracle. Larry Ellison hired Lane from consultancy Booz Allen Hamilton and tasked him with turning around the deeply troubled sales and marketing organizations. His efforts ultimately contributed to a tenfold increase in sales, from $1 billion to more than $10 billion, and a threefold increase in net profits. Similarly, AirTran CEO Joe Leonard recruited COO Robert Fornaro to lead a dramatic turnaround. The company, in Leonard's words, was 'running on fumes' and needed dramatic efforts to stave off bankruptcy.

Correct. The central pillar to a banking COO's capabilities – and the skill-set that could make or break this person's tenancy as COO – is managing and driving change and, indeed, taking this effort to the point of quantifiable benefit. This is not, however, limited to the 'strategic' as outlined above. While it is certainly important, so too is the COO's willingness to embrace operational and sometimes granular change programmes or projects. Whether the COO is managing a programme of work that will help the bank run more efficiently using its existing resources (more commonly referred to as 'run the bank' activities) or managing structural or strategic change ('change the bank' activities), having a proven ability in transformation is a critical attribute for any banking COO.

The mentor

Some companies bring a COO on board to mentor a young or inexperienced CEO (often a founder). A rapidly growing entrepreneurial venture might seek an industry veteran with seasoning, wisdom, and a rich network who can develop both the CEO and the emerging business. One could logically hypothesize that as the CEO develops, this COO role might either disappear or be heavily restructured.

By many accounts, this was what prompted the young Michael Dell to hire Mort Topfer in 1994. Dell was growing at a pace that threatened to get ahead of its founder's managerial experience. Michael Dell was self-aware enough to acknowledge that he needed some seasoned executives around, both to capitalize on the market opportunity and to accelerate his own development as a leader. Topfer was in his mid-fifties at the time and was completing a successful career at Motorola. He clearly had no aspirations of becoming the chief executive officer at Dell—he was there to help the 29-year-old Michael. We've seen very similar arrangements at Netscape, where James Barksdale has served as mentor to cofounder Marc Andreessen, and at Google, where Eric Schmidt was recruited to support the cofounders, Larry Page and Sergey Brin.

No, not in a preordained or defined manner. It is difficult to think of an example in banking when this mentoring role has been openly performed. It is true that many newly appointed CEO's rely heavily on well-established COOs – those perhaps with many more years' commercial experience. However, this is often a case of the CEO benefiting from the institutional knowledge of an inherited COO rather than the CEO perceiving the COO in a mentoring capacity, helping to develop and fine-tune her or his leadership skills. It is more likely that COOs find themselves in mentoring and cultivating roles for tomorrow's leaders. They may well lend an ear to some of the more junior business heads (perhaps even at the instigation of the CEO), but it is more likely that the COO devotes any mentoring time to the rising leadership within her or his COO and business management function.

The other half

A company may bring in a COO not as a mentor, but as a foil, to complement the CEO's experience, style, knowledge base, or penchants. Observers have viewed the relationships between Bill Gates and two of his previous COOs, Jon Shirley and Michael Hallman, in this light. Jon Shirley, according to one observer, provided a 'calm, self-effacing balance' to Gates's brilliant and often intimidating affect. In such cases, the COO role is usually not meant to lead to a higher position—but sometimes it is. When Ken Freeman, now a managing director of Kohlberg Kravis Roberts, was CEO at Corning spin-off Quest Diagnostics, he deliberately sought an heir with a different collection of skills than his. He ultimately hired Surya Mohapatra just when Quest was closing a deal to acquire another large testing business. 'I thought, in a company that was going from $1.5 billion in revenues to $3.2 billion,' he explained to us, 'it would be helpful to have somebody around that had strong health care experience—especially given that I had grown up in the glass business!'

This is a cornerstone of the assessment and selection process: the COO and CEO must together make a whole, their skill-sets complementary and well honed, their ambitions aligned and not in competition. Where the CEO lacks proven capability, interest or time, the COO's abilities, focus and allocation of time and effort should fill this gap. Certainly "in such cases, the COO role is usually not meant to lead to a higher position", as we have already described. Playing 'second fiddle' is a position to be embraced and celebrated by a COO in this context, a choice they make knowingly. They are the 'foil' – the equivalent of the ADC, the right hand to a senior military officer – and can be the sounding board, the quiet voice of reason, the calmness marrying well to the bravado and bombastic confidence possessed by many leaders, the communicator of policy, the go-to person to get things done.

Perhaps this point is best understood by looking at the literal meaning of the word 'foil' as defined in the Oxford Dictionary: "Foil: a person or thing that contrasts with and so emphasizes and enhances the qualities of another."

> *"My role is to take away the noise from the head of the business; to undertake many tasks he will never know I have done; to execute his vision and ensure in doing so that he looks good and is bulletproof in this process. To this end I am his foil, advisor, protector, junior business partner and confidante."*
>
> GLOBAL COO, RATES AND FX

The partner

Sometimes, the CEO is simply the kind of person who works best with a partner. This can lead to what's been called a 'two in a box' model and is similar to what authors David Heenan and Warren Bennis have termed 'co-leadership.' Indeed, Heenan and Bennis contend that more companies should create and cultivate co-leadership arrangements. But it's probably true that, just as there are doubles specialists in tennis, only some executives are more effective when paired. In any case, Michael Dell and Kevin Rollins, whom Dell introduced as COO in 1996, seem to operate in this mode. Dell, as chairman, and Rollins, now as CEO, are committed to leading the firm together, even choosing to 'co-office' in adjoining work spaces separated by only a glass partition.

The partnering scenario is highly relevant to the banking COO. Many banking COOs have their office next to their 'manager', with a glass petition separating them. They feel this physical arrangement – having the COO close by and visible – is a necessity, as banking is prone to immediacy and dynamic changing circumstances. 'Partnering' is not likely to follow the evolutionary process of Michael Dell and Kevin Rollins, with a CEO moving to become chairman and the COO being promoted to CEO. What does occur frequently in banking, however, is the COO following her or his manager as the latter secures promotion. In this scenario the COO is valued highly by the business head:

> *"My COO knows me inside-out, knows how I work, how best to work with me and navigates a path to ensure our skills are best utilised and have become perfectly complementary. It helps an awful lot that we get on, are not friends outside*

work, but have a chemistry, sharing common values, a common sense of humour and a joint ambition to be the best at what we do."

FIXED INCOME BUSINESS HEAD

The quote above offers an interesting insight, as it insinuates that their competencies have become complementary, a by-product of time and working together, as opposed to this complementary fit being understood or known at the outset. It takes time to cultivate a successful CEO-COO working partnership, and having a joint ambition encourages a strong partnership that works towards success. Head of fixed income is a senior (and serious) executive role in banking, but the ambition for this business head would perhaps be to become CEO one day (of markets), and his or her COO would see this as a path to becoming the COO to the CEO of markets. The risk in this strategy for the COO is nailing their colours to the mast of their present manager, for if they fall out of favour, the COO is left exposed. There are examples where the loss of a career patron has been detrimental and damaging to further career advancement.

The heir apparent

In many cases, the primary reason to establish a COO position is to groom—or test—a company's CEO-elect. The broad purview of the job allows an heir apparent to learn the whole company: its business, environment, and people. Recent examples of firms using the COO position to develop the successor to the CEO include Continental Airlines, where CEO Gordon Bethune (who himself originally joined the airline as COO) recently passed the torch to his COO, Larry Kellner. Similarly, in the time after Rex Tillerson was appointed to the number two position at Exxon, observers noted that he was increasingly exposed to the public—a deliberate effort to facilitate his succession to CEO Lee Raymond. And when Norfolk Southern appointed Charles Moorman as second in command, the transportation company touted him as the heir, continuing its avowed 'practice of picking an executive young enough to lead the company for at least a decade.'

Certainly, being identified as a likely heir does not represent anything approaching a guarantee. On the one hand, an otherwise valuable senior executive may leave if the top job ultimately goes to someone else—or isn't offered soon enough. On the other hand, the COO's performance can indicate that the heir title was inappropriately or prematurely bestowed. In the past few years, we've seen several prominent COOs who seemed to be on the glide path to the CEO's office instead leave their companies; they include John Brock (Cadbury Schweppes), Mike Zafirovski (Motorola), John Walter (AT&T), and Robert Willumstad (Citigroup). Regardless of whether each left because he was passed over for the CEO position, because the timing was not as advertised, or because he found greener pastures, the succession plan unravelled.

Within banking, and specifically within the financial markets, the COO is rarely (if ever) appointed as the 'heir apparent'. The skill-set and experiences of banking COOs are matched with the tasks for which they will be responsible, not based on their potential as a business leader. As such, you would not assess a potential COO on any future need for them to deal directly with clients and investors, or on their experience in aspects of business risk management. However, you would assess them directly and – my experience suggests – solely on being able to do the job at hand, namely that of the COO.

If a markets' COO has been appointed from within the business, that person is supported by a Chief Administrative Officer (CAO). This appears to be window dressing, to allow the position of COO to be used as a stepping stone to career progression, or perhaps offered as emotional compensation if a senior member of the business has lost out in the fight for promotion elsewhere. The CAO becomes the buffer and the executor of most of the tasks in the COO's in-tray, as the CAO will have the relevant skills to deliver on these tasks. This of course means that the COO is not directly exposed to the minutiae of the role, and in reality the CAO is the COO in all but title.

The MVP

Finally, some companies offer the job of COO as a promotion to an executive considered too valuable to lose, particularly to a competitor. This appears to have been the case at News Corporation's Fox Entertainment Group subsidiary. It recently announced that its president and COO, Peter Chernin, had signed a new employment agreement preventing a rumored move to rival Disney. Similarly, when McDonald's restructured the roles of its U.S. and Europe presidents during the summer of 2004, that was interpreted by analysts as an effort to ward off poachers. With this strategy, an organization may try to hedge its bets by stopping short of identifying a specific heir or setting a timetable for leadership succession, in an effort to keep its high-potential executives intrigued about what the future might hold for them, should they stay on board.

This does not appear to be a type of COO, but how you can use the appointment to achieve a specific, non-core business-related objective. Using the role as 'emotional compensation' or as a 'sweetener' is a tactical rather than strategic use of the role. It may well fulfil the short-term need to keep a specific senior person happy, but this only parks the problem. More importantly, it sends a confused message to the business about how the position of the COO is perceived and valued. Those who have dedicated their careers to business management and to advancement within the COO community may see this tactical use of the position as disrespectful. They will know that the appointee does not have the prerequisite skills to be successful in the role and that company politics has played a part. This is particularly the case where a CAO is appointed and becomes responsible for fulfilling the COO's responsibilities.

Elusive lessons

In truth, as we've said, the seven roles are not mutually exclusive. Though it's hard to imagine a single person wearing several of these hats all at once, it's quite possible that a COO could wear two of them simultaneously. Understanding the roles distinctly, however, and considering their differences reveal a few things clearly.

First, the typology we've outlined makes it easy to see why COOs have been hard to investigate in any scientific sense. Even where studies have been done, it's often impossible to draw useful lessons from them. For example, one of the few empirical examinations of the role was conducted by Donald Hambrick of Penn State and Albert Cannella, Jr., when he was at Texas A&M. As they reported in the October 2004 issue of Strategic Management Journal, a review of ten years of data on 400 companies showed that firms with a CEO-COO structure had underperformed relative to their industry peers. It's a provocative finding, but its implications are far from apparent. Is the structure itself to blame? Or was a COO hired to compensate for a weak CEO? Put another way, is the COO part of the problem or part of the solution? Hambrick and Cannella offered both explanations, and other theories could be constructed. Our work suggests that divining answers from such broad surveys is inherently difficult because the nature of the COO job is so deeply contextual.

Second, knowing the variety of roles that COOs play sheds light on the phenomenon of the 'vanishing COO.' Some observers, counting the instances of companies declining to fill vacated COO spots, have concluded that the position is headed for extinction. After a COO departs, it often appears that his or her duties have been divided up among top managers without much disruption. When Steve Heyer left Coca-Cola, his responsibilities were dispersed in this fashion, and the position was not filled. When COO Gary Daichendt left Nortel Networks (after just three months), his tasks were assumed by the then CEO, Bill Owens. But the job is oftentimes reinstated or created in a company that didn't use it before. At Microsoft, for example, rumors of the COO job's death turned out to have been exaggerated. Although it sat idle for several years after Rick Belluzzo's departure, it was revived when Kevin Turner was hired.

Finally, the tremendous variation in COO roles and responsibilities manifestly implies that there is no standard set of 'great COO' attributes. This makes finding suitable candidates difficult for executive recruiters (as one of the authors can attest). More important, it stymies the CEOs and boards who must select among the candidates. The existence of seven different roles suggests at least seven different sets of attributes on top of the basic—and infinitely variable—requirement that there exist a personal chemistry between the COO and the current CEO.

In this book we investigate the evolving role of the banking COO and, more specifically, the COO within markets. The paper we are quoting from here, written in 2006, is a retrospective view on the role and situational circumstance of the COO, but research suggests that outside banking, much of what the paper summarises so succinctly and supports with extensive market examples, remains the same. Since 2006, however, banking has experienced the genesis and evolution of the COO role, followed by a period of reflection and then one of further evolution. The banking COO is here to stay, but is changing to meet the demands placed on it –

unlike the suggestion above that the COO role is struggling to find its footing and may be 'facing extinction'.

There are a variety of COO roles within banking, but at heart they are similar from one bank to another. While some COOs could move from outside banking to an aligned business – within an asset management company or a hedge fund, for example – they remain in the broader financial services sector. Therefore, a standard set of attributes arguably exists for the role of the COO within the banking sector. What differentiates the role is that it is not the springboard to promotion to lead the business, which might lead to potential jealousies that could inhibit the COO-CEO relationship. With this in mind, the COO selection process is based on a well-framed technical skill-set and demonstrable experience. Perhaps more challenging is finding the 'right' person with a personality that will work with that of the hiring manager and influence how quickly trust can be built.

The underpinnings of success

Even though the role is so contingent, we have identified some success factors that came up consistently in our interviews with executives in widely varying situations. The single element most critical to the success of a CEO-COO pairing, we quickly saw, is the level of trust between the two individuals. To speak of trust is almost a cliché, but the vehemence with which our research participants stressed it suggests they consider it more crucial here than in any other business relationship. Wendell Weeks, who rose from COO to CEO at Corning, referred to the need for a 'true partnership, in every sense of the word.' The trust has to be absolute, he said, 'because there are those in the organization who are always seeking to drive wedges if they can.' Other executives specifically used the metaphor of having one another's back. Hearing their comments, we were reminded of Harry Levinson's insightful 1993 article, 'Between CEO and COO,' in the Academy of Management Executive. In it, he wrote, 'The relationship…is fraught with many psychological complexities. Perhaps it is the most difficult of all organizational working relationships because more than others, it is a balancing act on the threshold of power.' Levinson went on to explore the dysfunctions that can arise in such situations: unhealthy rivalries, defensiveness, over-control, rigidity, misconceptions, and doubt.

How can a pair of executives get past such perils and develop an extraordinary level of trust? Again, consistent themes in our interviews suggest the answer. The CEO must feel certain that the COO shares the vision, is not gunning for the top spot, and can get the job done. Conversely, the COO must be sure that the CEO will provide whatever is needed to do the job, will not put any obstacles in the way, and will not thwart future career advancement. Let's explore this question more fully, framing it in terms of what each party owes the other.

Trust lies at the heart of any COO-CEO relationship. The bridge of confidence between two people operating together with separate yet united agendas is essential for this relationship to work. One must presume this trust is in place from day one, but it is also earned and reinforced with time and consistent delivery. From the start a level of trust exists from a professional perspective – an expectation that comes with the rank and responsibility, from prior experience which sets levels of expectation. With time this trust becomes deeper and stronger. Trust goes hand in hand with reliability; reliability is based on a consistent record of delivery and is enhanced by effective and on going communication between the two parties.

What the COO owes the CEO

True respect

Because a chief executive relies so heavily on the second in command to accomplish mission-critical goals, it's essential that the COO wholeheartedly believe in the CEO's strategic leadership. Chief operating officers, by virtue of their inherent talents and their organizational position, are highly visible and powerful. If the COO is not aligned with the CEO's vision, or not convinced that the CEO can find the best path forward, then that lieutenant is capable of real mischief. Dan Rosensweig, COO at Yahoo, described for us the hours he spent talking with CEO Terry Semel before joining the company. Rosensweig invested the time because, in his words, 'you have to get in sync with the CEO. If you have an agenda that is different than his or hers, you will absolutely fail the company.'

An ego in check

In the interviews we conducted—particularly those with COOs—we heard repeatedly how critical it is for seconds in command to check their egos at the door. It's a tricky balance to achieve, given that COOs must obviously be self-confident leaders. 'You have to lead while serving,' stressed eBay COO Maynard Webb, immediately adding, 'It has been the hardest job that I have ever done.' Interestingly, he then followed up with another reason why the job is hard: 'It is not as immediate with gratification as any of the line jobs that I had. When you are solving technology issues, such as is the site up or not, it is pretty black and white, and you see some of the results pretty quickly. But you are working on things through a lot more layers as COO, and the results come much slower.' These sound like two very different reasons for a job to be hard, but we suspect they may be intertwined. Often, the results do come more slowly—and often they come in a way that makes their proper attribution more difficult to discern. Regardless, the COO is not necessarily in line to receive the kudos for a job well done.

An eye on execution

Back in the 1990s, people in organizations jokingly picked up on a phrase from the television series Star Trek: The Next Generation. In it, starship captain Jean-Luc Picard, having settled on a course of action, would simply instruct his crew to 'make it so.' CEOs in general can't quite get away with that, but to the extent that they are focused on strategy, they rely on COOs to oversee much of the implementation. They must be able to trust that they can afford to address longer-term and bigger-picture issues because their second in command will maintain a focus on the here and now. Even COOs who are not primarily playing the executor role should have an execution mindset and a bias toward action.

Coaching and coordination skills

A COO must be able to direct and coach others throughout the business. Steven Reinemund, now chairman and CEO at PepsiCo, gave us his thoughts on the challenge. He was promoted to COO after having led a business unit and, he told us, 'I had to think long and hard about whether I really wanted to move out of running the day-to-day business into a role where I coach and coordinate.' Being a division president, he explained, 'is a hands-on job. You get to mold the strategy; you get to direct the efforts every day. You have the functional people that you work with, and that team performs against a mission, and it is an exciting experience.' The COO job, by contrast, requires an individual who 'can step out of doing day-to-day, hands-on directing and leading of a business, and direct and teach and coach others.' Again, regardless of which of the seven roles a COO plays, the CEO must be able to trust that these skills are in place.

Communication

The COOs we spoke with understood that the onus was on them to embrace the CEO's strategy and work to make it real. But no one can execute against a plan that's not being communicated clearly and directly. CEOs constantly have fresh thoughts with operational implications; they must be in the habit of discussing those with their COOs without delay. Ken Freeman told us how he and Surya Mohapatra kept the lines of communication active at Quest Diagnostics. 'Sunday at 4:00 pm became the time for us to have lengthy discussions....We would see each other at the office, too, of course, but there we would be scurrying around working on the integration of the [merged] companies, driving the company's performance, and making things go. We had each other's undivided attention via telephone starting at 4:00, virtually every single Sunday for five years.' Another CEO we interviewed admitted an early mistake: locating his new COO's office in a separate building, thereby failing to capitalize on the rich communication afforded by physical proximity.

CEOs constantly have fresh thoughts with operational implications; they must be in the habit of discussing those with their COOs without delay.

Clear decision rights

To a person, the executives we interviewed stressed the need for explicit and reasonable lines of demarcation between CEO and COO responsibilities. While there was no consensus on what exactly should be part of each job, everyone agreed that the matter had to be sorted out at the start of the relationship. It's far easier to delineate boundaries when the two individuals clearly have complementary competencies and each naturally gravitates to different areas of expertise. The greater the overlap in competencies, the greater the likelihood that the COO might feel (perhaps accurately) that the CEO is micromanaging and second-guessing decisions. Such behavior on the part of the CEO communicates to the COO a lack of trust that is likely to engender friction in the relationship. When we raised this point with Bob Herbold, another former COO at Microsoft, he responded: 'To me, this is a key issue. The way it gets worked out is the individuals—through trial and error, as well as through discussions—figure out who is going to be doing what and who needs to check with who on key decisions….How the pair will make that happen needs to be agreed to very early in the relationship.'

A lock on the back door

Obviously, the creation of the COO role adds a layer of management; executives who previously had direct access to the CEO now have an intermediary to address. One of the COO's first challenges is to develop relationships with direct reports that discourage them from seeking backdoor access to the CEO. At the same time, the COO must depend on the CEO to block efforts by those who might want to circumvent the position. This is not to say that restricting access to the CEO is the goal. Ed Zander, now CEO of Motorola, previously served as COO of Sun Microsystems under Scott McNealy. Zander says the two made it clear that any of the COO's direct reports was entitled to go to McNealy to talk about things. But the lines of responsibility were still respected. 'One thing that Scott did very well was to never undermine me,' Zander told us. 'He always backed all my decisions. He would hear people out but then send them to me.'

A number of the people we interviewed noted how much personal discipline is required on the CEO's part to maintain this kind of line. 'I have been working on nailing that back door shut for a while,' eBay COO Webb told us. 'I think it is a tough, tough thing to do, especially when you have a CEO that actually loves to get involved in problem solving and wants to help. I think what you have to do in that case is to enable, not control, communication and be transparent.'

A shared spotlight

Without exception, the COOs we interviewed accepted the fact that their job was to make the CEO successful—and that in doing so they in many ways rendered their own contributions less visible. But, especially for COOs who aspire to the top job, that creates a dilemma. Jim Donald, president and CEO of Starbucks, noted that what gets executives to the role of president and COO 'won't necessarily earn them a CEO role. Once you are in the COO role, you have to…broaden the network of things you do. You need to work with the board, work with the CEO, and work to lead others to be successful.'

It falls upon the CEO's shoulders to make sure that this development takes place and to share the spotlight whenever appropriate. If the CEO is not deliberate about this, then the board will have no reason to be impressed by the number two, who may then prove ultimately unpromotable. Kevin Sharer, who was COO at Amgen before he became CEO, lays heavy emphasis on this point. He told us that the success of the CEO-COO relationship is '75% dependent on a few things that the CEO does.' He framed those things for us as a series of important questions:

Does the CEO give the number two real authority, real operating responsibility, power that is real, power that is seen by the rest of the company as real? Second, does the number one actually encourage and let the number two person have his or her own voice in board meetings and operating reviews? Third, does the CEO give coaching, counselling, and really see the success of the number two as part of the company's success?

"What the COO owes the CEO" is a statement, but based on the extract above it should be turned into a question – perhaps a rhetorical one. If you step back and look at any relationship, in or out of commerce and the workplace, the fundamentals that make it work are trust, communication, respect, interdependence, honesty and acknowledgement. The 'hand-in-glove' nature of the CEO-

COO relationship means that all these factors must be there to make it work. Like any relationship, investing time with each other up front does not guarantee success or longevity, but it does enhance the chances of them. This is confirmed by Dan Rosensweig, former COO at Yahoo, as he "described for us the hours he spent talking with CEO Terry Semel before joining the company".

It is thus surprising how little time some banking business heads spend directly with their potential COO before extending an offer of employment. They tend to undertake an introductory interview (some even get an internal third party to do this initial screening), then socialise preferred candidates through peer and peer-plus-one interviews. They rarely allocate adequate time to get to know the person they are about to appoint – arguably their most important team member. The flip side of this is that prospective hires appear to be happy with this superficial selection process and take a leap of faith based more on their self-appreciation of the role and the steadfastness of the company they are about to join than on a focused assessment of the person with which they are agreeing to work.

In banking, 'ego' is an attribute that has had plenty of media attention, and much of this is deserved. In my experience as an executive search consultant, the best relationships are built with those who respect what I do and my ability to find the best person for them. The clients understand the importance of partnering their search consultant to understand exactly what they are looking for and do what is necessary to expedite the process. The banking industry, however, still sadly includes a small pocket of self-important senior managers. It is generally these people who struggle with the hiring process, as they have a poor reputation in this small marketplace, and they rarely spend the necessary time with the search consultant up front or in communication within the process to find success.

There have been a number of occasions in recent years when such senior managers have found themselves out of work, redundant, some coming cap in hand looking for help. Some take the fall graciously and develop the necessary humility to find success in the future. Others do not. Such egos have no place in modern banking, where conduct, integrity and decent human behaviour are expected of the industry's leaders.

Finding someone who can keep their ego in check, understanding the need to 'lead while serving', is therefore key to the behavioural assessment undertaken by the search consultant and the interview panel. Similarly, much of what a COO does goes unnoticed. Often it is not until business heads lose their COO that they realise the innumerable tasks – some of them menial – the COO performed without seeking acknowledgement. A good COO can wait for the mid to long term to see their efforts come to fruition.

This is also relevant to the CEO's attitude. "They must be able to trust that they can afford to address longer-term and bigger-picture issues because their second in command will maintain a focus on the here and now." This is more important than ever in banking, when the immediate demands of the regulators and the dynamic nature of the banking industry means that the COO is the executive resource dedicated to keeping the business operating day in and day out, while paying secondary reference to the mid- to long term. The long-term strategy, the CEO's vision and its execution, however, will be passed to the COO. Juggling the two demands is a skill the COO must possess to be successful.

"I had to think long and hard about whether I really wanted to move out of running the day-to-day business into a role where I coach and coordinate." This extract from the article is not so relevant to the considerations of most career business managers and COOs, as talent management has been a principal responsibility within various roles leading the COO appointment. This is an area in which they have proven capabilities as well as a deep-rooted interest. The COO job, by contrast, requires an individual who 'doing day-to-day, hands-on directing and leading of a business, and direct and teach and coach others."

What the CEO owes the COO is time: time dedicated to making their relationship work; time allocated to developing effective communication channels between the two, where often in banking their offices are separated by only a glass panel to "capitalise on the rich communication afforded by physical proximity"; time up front and ongoing to ensure 'clear decision rights' are understood and allocated. The banking industry and its leaders are generally good at such commitment, as the need to provide it drives this dedicated approach. Within banking, where the career COO is well established, delineation of responsibilities between the CEO and COO is required and usually agreed at the outset, ensuring each can deliver within demanding, often highly visible roles, whether internally and externally.

Much of the above can be achieved up front through an effective hiring process, and this investment in time will pay dividends. Making sure that both parties understand there are aspects of ambiguity, with changing boundaries, will help both cross these hurdles when they arise – but only if supported by active post-appointment communication, which should lead to the two working in a complementary fashion. As Bob Herbold, a former COO at Microsoft, notes above: "To me, this is a key issue. The way it gets worked out is the individuals – through trial and error, as well as through discussions – figure out who is going to be doing what and who needs to check with who on key decisions….How the pair will make that happen needs to be agreed to very early in the relationship."

This relationship is helped hugely if the CEO is clear in his or hercommunication and support of the COO role and where it sits in the hierarchy. Supporting the COO at all times, despite the undoubted challengers to the CEO's authority, is key to the sustainability and authority of the banking COO, especially as so much depends on the person's influencing skills, leveraging the indirect authority gifted to them through the CEO. This is made more complicated in many banks – notorious for their politics – where product and business lines vie for influence and attention as much as the regions and locations. 'Locking the back door' to not always well-meaning managers seeking an audience with the CEO or head of business is a constant challenge for any COO, but even more so for the banking COO: "One of the COO's first challenges is to develop relationships with direct reports that discourage them from seeking backdoor access to the CEO. At the same time, the COO must depend on the CEO to block efforts by those who might want to circumvent the position." The skill-set required here is perfectly summarised as followed: "I think what you have to do in that case is to enable, not control, communication and be transparent."

As previously noted, difficulties can arise when equally powerful, influential and impactful leaders seek a share of the spotlight. This can be overcome, however, and the glory can be shared, when the CEO's recognition and taking the plaudits are externally oriented, as opposed to the COO, whose is likely to only gain internal praise. As banking COOs do not generally aspire to the top job, the fact that their contributions are not as visible as those of the CEO is less relevant. However, this does mean that the CEOs then face the difficulty of fulfilling their COO's career aspirations: 'What next?' is a question any COO is going to ask after they have been in this position for some time. Therefore, most – if not all – banking COOs would agree with the following statement in the article: "Without exception, the COOs we interviewed accepted the fact that their job was to make the CEO successful – and that in doing so they in many ways rendered their own contributions less visible. But, especially for COOs who aspire to the top job, that creates a dilemma." The three questions further raised also lend themselves to the analysis in another essay investigating the difference between COO and CAO (see page 83):

- Does the CEO give the number two real authority, real operating responsibility, power that is real, power that is seen by the rest of the company as real?
- Second, does the number one actually encourage and let the number two person have his or her own voice in board meetings and operating reviews?
- Third, does the CEO give coaching, counselling, and really see the success of the number two as part of the company's success?

A role on the rise?

Ask anyone who has worked as or alongside a COO—the job is demanding. Now we know it's unique, as well. Perhaps that's why COO is the only C-suite title to which there is no magazine devoted. It's a trivial observation but perhaps a telling one; the common set of issues and interests that would imply simply does not exist.

Is it a role in decline? Some observers, as we have said, certainly think so. The Hambrick and Cannella study, for example, found a 22% decline over ten years in the number of firms with executives holding that title. Yet in the last few years, companies in a wide range of industries have announced new COOs, including Microsoft, RadioShack, Airbus, Allstate, KPMG's U.S. subsidiary, Alcatel, Chiron, Nissan, BellSouth, Comcast, Eli Lilly, Apple, and Medtronic.

We can easily argue that there is a growing need for the role. First, consider the widening scope of the CEO's job. Today, we have bigger companies, with expanding global operations, aggressively pursuing acquisitions. CEOs are asked to be public figures, communicating with many constituencies at the same time that increasingly democratic and knowledge-based organizations require them to spend a great deal of time campaigning internally for any change they hope to make. Second, companies are becoming more deliberate about succession planning. Boards are anxious to identify and groom heirs and often see the COO title as a useful step in the process. Finally, the easy mobility of top talent means companies must find ways to hold on to their most valuable non-CEO executives. The COO title can be effective in staving off wanderlust.

In light of these trends, it's surprising that COOs are not more common. Our suspicion is that they would be if there were less variability and confusion surrounding the role. Board members aren't sure when the position will add value. Recruiters don't have an obvious pool to tap. CEOs don't know whom to trust. Potential COOs don't know whether the job is right for them. This is why it's vital to build on the work we've outlined here. As we continue to demystify the role of the COO, more companies will benefit from more effective leadership.

The rise of the COO

Does your company have a COO today? What role does he or she play in the organization? Does your COO have the best shot at becoming the next CEO? The answers may not be as self-evident as many executives think.

That's what we found when we studied the top management teams of companies in Europe over the past three years. Few European companies have COOs, although their numbers appear to be growing. Of the 97 largest listed companies in the UK and the Eurozone in 2010, only 37 had a COO in their executive ranks.

Appointing a COO is a recent trend on the continent. Only two of the 37 organizations we studied had appointed more than two COOs in their history; in 27, the current COOs had only one predecessor; and in the remaining eight corporations, the incumbents were the companies' first COOs. COOs are relatively common in service industries such as financial services, energy, information technology and telecommunications, but in manufacturing sectors — such as automotive, chemical, and pharmaceutical companies — they are relatively rare.

Most COOs in Europe are seasoned executives; they were 48 years old, on average, when they were appointed. There was quite a range, though: the youngest in our sample was 32 years old when he became COO, while the oldest three took office at the age of 58.

There appears to be a correlation between age and tenure; executives usually needed to be veterans of the same company if they were to become COOs. The COOs in our sample had worked in the same company for 12 years, on average, before their appointment. A majority of companies — 33 of 37, to be precise — recruited COOs internally.

COOs in Europe are, distressingly, predominantly male, with only one female COO in the companies we studied. Part of the problem may be in the backgrounds that companies desired: 85% of COOs had experience in operations, strategy, or finance. In several industries, such as consumer goods, financial services, industrial products, and logistics, COOs usually had backgrounds in either managing operations or information technology departments. Almost half of the COOs we studied had business degrees and around a third had engineering degrees.

The COO's role, we find, is driven by three factors: the company's strategy, the composition of the executive team, and the relationships between the members of the top team. In contrast to previous studies, we didn't find evidence that the COO's role is determined entirely by the CEO.

With markets shrinking and cash flows declining, COOs have built their credibility in most companies by focusing on operational efficiency and helping to meet their margin goals. This has helped improve their standing; COOs are increasingly becoming responsible for rolling out transformation agendas.

It still doesn't seem necessary to be a COO in order to take over as CEO, though. When we analyzed the careers of all the incumbent CEOs of the companies in our sample, we found that only 23 of them had previously been COOs. But, with COOs increasingly landing key assignments because the office lies at the intersection of strategy and operations, we feel that not promoting them to the top job may be a missed opportunity. What do you think?

The investigation into the role of the COO above is interesting and relevant, as it demonstrates largely how the COO role, if used correctly, can be empowered to enhance the CEO's ability to do his or her job and, if operated in a true partnership, benefits both parties, with the real beneficiary the company itself.

Within banking, the role is no longer on the rise – it has arisen and is embedded as a key leadership role within almost all banking companies. If anything, there are now too many COOs by title, which has led to a dilution of significance of the title (although this is being addressed by some banks). What is more important is that the role is a recognised mandate of authority at the top table, which the new regulatory era has ensured.

What echoes from the past within these closing comments is the paragraph that states: "With markets shrinking and cash flows declining, COOs have built their credibility in most companies by focusing on operational efficiency and helping to meet their margin goals. This has helped improve their standing; COOs are increasingly becoming responsible for rolling out transformation agendas." This is the same scenario in which the banking industry and its COOs find themselves today, some ten years on from when this article was written. 'Transformation' is a key skill for all COOs, where change and the change agenda are driven almost without exception by two things: a) cost and b) regulatory change. With falling revenues, most industry's leaders would say this challenge alone is enough, but coupled with an intensive and highly intrusive regulatory agenda, the strength of the industry's COO cadre is under severe scrutiny. COOs will largely be responsible for navigating the industry through these stormy seas to calmer waters. So how do we conclude our thoughts on the role of the banking COO versus that of the COO outside it?

"Does your company have a COO today?" Yes, too many, but through time and endeavour the role will be further defined. It is the cornerstone of any bank's leadership team, where no defined route to appointment exists, but a common framework of skills and experiences is evolving that matches the demands of the role today.

"What role does he or she play in the organisation? Does your COO have the best shot at becoming the next CEO?" No, hardly ever, and that is not the intention. Unless supported by a CAO carrying out the COO role in practise, the role of the banking COO demands a very different skill-set. More junior COOs can and perhaps should be used as staging posts for the future business heads, but the executive COO, whether group or more specifically the markets' COO, should follow a career path through many of the bank's key areas of operation, not limited to roles focused on and judged by revenue creation.

"With COOs increasingly landing key assignments because the office lies at the intersection of strategy and operations, we feel that not promoting them to the top job may be a missed opportunity." This is a confident and forceful conclusion. But it misses the point of the banking COO, as the career business manager or COO rightly perceives that being appointed the global COO is the top job, the top job within the career they have pursued and a position to which hundreds or even thousands aspire. If understood, then the only missed opportunity is where business heads or CEOs fail to understand how to select, hire, manage and develop the right relationship with their COO to maximise individual, collective and corporate success.

香港龜苓膏
香港龜苓膏 · 甜品
For Lease

善
公司
COMPANY
32号
華安
CHOP WAH ON
Established
1916年成立
華安 CHOP WAH ON
SINCE 1916
TEL: 6223 4349 FAX: 6221 4140
www.chopwahon.com
華安

"Career management and advancement are now the primary reason for the movement of COOs, and the entry point and the career opportunity are balanced against a feeling that many have found themselves in a career cul-de-sac."

CAREER PROGRESSION AS A COO

A theoretical and moral requirement or practical impossibility?

Career management and how best to develop talent within the COO function have been the subjects of debate within banking for years. It is a question that anyone advancing a career within business management will ask themselves on occasion – and it is one that appears to offer no clear answer.

With the changing role of the COO and the growth of opportunities in business management since 2008, this subject demands investigation. To this end, I conducted back-to-back forums in London and New York in quarter four 2015 with over 50 COOs from 20 banks. The debate was a hearty one, and armed with this cross-industry, transatlantic representation, I was able to gain an insight into this complex subject. The findings outlined below are in themselves representative of market-wide opinion.

The debate was set as follows:

Talent management within front-office business management

Fostering the future leadership of the markets' COO community

How do you identify and develop today's talent to become the commercial COO managing directorate of tomorrow?

The debate addressed the following questions:

1 What are the key/common components of the managing director, COO role today?

2 What are the common/required behavioural and technical competencies to be successful in this role?

3 Concluding 1 and 2, what therefore makes the difference between the competent and valued, but limited (e.g., lifetime director), and the one who can break through and establish him or herself at the higher level?

4 Can these competencies be used to frame selection of a VP (this will vary bank to bank, but targeted 10 years [+] commercial experience), as an entry into the business management community?

5 What talent pools might therefore be accessible/leveraged to source this VP talent?

6 How and what path could a VP entry hire be managed through to MD to produce the commercially competent executive COO?

One COO set the tone of the debate from the outset:

> *"Whilst I could summarise my thoughts in detail and talk for many an hour on this subject, having navigated my own career through business management for over twenty-five years, my short summary at this stage is that simply we do not have a uniform and/or structured approach*

to career management within the COO and/or business management community. We have tried to make one work, but such attempts seem to frustrate the ad hoc, meritocratic and opportunist career advancement which is at the heart of any career within business management. You make your own career, choose your patrons carefully, promote yourself, but define yourself by getting things done. The latter is your passport to career advancement."

This proved to be a far-reaching statement at the beginning of the debate, encapsulating the opinions of most of the attendees. The conversations of the debates led to a majority conclusion that it was not achievable to do so, despite the desire of senior management to hold and to be held responsible for the career development of their staff. This group of senior managers all recognised that they should have such a programme of investment, but despite their sense of duty, it had been impossible to deliver (although many had invested time and effort in attempting to implement it).

Why? The nature of the role, its immediacy and dynamic nature embedded in the business management function made it very difficult – if not impossible – to outline a defined career path for those entering at VP level, or indeed those directors with ambitions to achieve MD status. Those entering this function have to understand the dynamic. Similarly, the selection of those being brought into the business management function should in no small part be based on their behavioural attributes and the ability to accept that they will have to navigate their own path to success. As another COO put it:

"This path will often be found within a state of continual flux, unforeseen opportunity and ambiguity. Indeed, to be successful, you will need to be able to thrive in an unstructured environment and understand that career progression and mobility are, in equal measure, resting in your hands to those of your manager; where delivery, patronage and personality will weigh evenly when tipping the scales of opportunity."

In good times, it was noted, career advancement was not as important, because industry growth offered opportunity and good markets provided excellent financial reward. In more challenging times, however, reduced opportunities for advancement and plateauing compensation caused many to turn their attention to career advancement.

Since 2012 and more so since the 2016 depressed bonus round, upper-quartile talent within business management has been looking more earnestly at the mid to long term, and this is stoking the fire of movement from one bank to another for different reasons. While the market is compressed, opportunities exist, as the COO function manoeuvres itself to meet the demands of the regulatory agenda, control, conduct, governance, front-to-back cost management and transformation.

Traditionally, motivations to move are as follows:

- Compensation.
- Loss of corporate allegiance.
- Direct management issues.
- Career advancement.

Career management and advancement are now the primary reason for the movement of COOs, and the entry point and the career opportunity are balanced against a feeling that many have found themselves in a career cul-de-sac. Career progression within the COO function – or the lack of it – is an issue for banks. Agreement on this fundamental point led to the question: "If there is no predetermined next step internally (and therefore a list of technical competencies and requirements attached to it), how do you assess someone for entry into the business management function or for promotion once established within it?"

Subject-matter expertise is clearly important, but the debate leaned towards the conclusion that it was not as important as when determining someone's suitability for other career moves within banking, such as within risk, technology, operations or even as a trader. Behavioural aspects were deemed to be equally, if not more, important when assessing and selecting those entering business management, as these are the skills that help someone navigate their own career, when no defined path is offered. The rising leaders of the COO function are looking for the following in career management:

- Clarity about how they will be assessed and what behavioural characteristics they must demonstrate, and how these will be measured.
- The opportunity to do so, to 'grandstand' their efforts, and to stand or fall through their delivery.

COO forum feedback

"If limited to four core technical and subject-matter competencies or experiences, what would they be?"

Person	Response 1	Response 2	Response 3	Response 4
A	Strong business commercial understanding	Financial management	Basel III expertise	E2E industry knowledge
B	Project management	Project expertise	Technology abilities	Markets expertise
C	Working in business	Risk and regulatory understanding	Audit experience	Front-to-back experience
D	Holistic understanding of front-to-back business and business processes	Appreciation of pressures the business is under to make its performance targets, but also the numerous cost constraints and so on placed on the control and support functions	Experience of strategic change delivery and tactical fixes	In the current environment, some experience of electronic trading
E	Program management (preferably evidencing ability to leverage others to get very many things done at the same time)	Asset class experience that demonstrates knowledge of end-to-end market structure (or a similar asset class with transferable skills)	Technical capital-related skills and knowledge	A good understanding of the global regulatory framework
F	Knowledge of markets products	Knowledge of markets process	Knowledge of IT and project management	Knowledge of compliance
G	Operational/risk/Control and or consultancy type background	Interest in financial markets	Excel and PowerPoint skills	Project management skills

"If limited to six behavioural attributes and competencies, what would they be?"

Person	Response 1	Response 2	Response 3	Response 4	Response 5	Response 6
A	Strong business commercial mindset	Strategic mindset	Strong interpersonal skills	Strong communication skills	Execution focused	Ability to deal with uncertain and chaotic/ changing priorities environment
B	Smart; fast learner	Ability to operate through virtual teams	Ability to develop relationships	Ability to prioritise and organise fluidly	Business analysis skills	Balance in decision-making
C	Emotional intelligence	Solutions focused	Strategic	Pragmatic	Thick skinned	Able to deal with high work volumes
D	Communication	Dependability	Stakeholder management	Time management	Openness	Collaborative
E	Strong analytical skills combined with being an excellent communicator; specifically an ability to distil complex multifaceted problems into a coherent strategy or plan for resolution	Ability to influence others beyond your direct management (up, down and across)	Integrity and fortitude; faces facts, willing to take personal risk to speak up (in any context), make decisions or do the right thing	A bias to execution; specifically a 'finisher' of projects and willing to get hands dirty as needed		
F	Adaptability	Change leader	Decision-maker	Team player		
G	Self-starter	Interpersonal and motivational	Good communication	Resiliency	Hard working	Adaptable

"What are the three questions you would use to assess the suitability of a potential COO hire, whether entry or established?"

Person	Response 1	Response 2	Response 3
A	What do you see as the key challenges for the industry/specific business?	How are you addressing those challenges as a leader in your organisation?	What examples do you have where you personally contributed to develop the top line?
B	Tell me your view of the critical industry trends right now and how these will play out over the next three to five years.	What do you see as the competitive advantages of the business unit we work in versus our competitor peers?	
C	What would your top three priorities be in the new role?	What would your previous bosses and colleagues say about you?	What would you change in the business strategy of this firm/business if you were boss for the day?
D	n/a	n/a	n/a
E	What is it about being a COO that motivates you to get up every morning and come into the office ready to deliver everything you have got?	What is the strategy of our investment bank, and how do you think the COO function plays a role in that? (Can be turned to ask about current employer if feeling kinder.)	Give me three examples of recent regulation that was a good idea.
F	If you were the 'big boss', how would you organise these different functions: FO supervision and control, COO, IT and operations?	How would you change the culture of the trading rooms?	How would you go 'full electronic' with small clients/tickets?
G	Describe a situation in which you had to influence multiple stakeholders to prioritise a new system build and implementation.	Give me an example of when you felt a control incident or risk issue had occurred and needed to be escalated. How did you manage the situation both internally and externally?	How do you assess top talent and build a strong team?

Role description

COO Financial Markets, Wholesale Bank

JOB TITLE	JOB GRADE	GENERIC JOB ROLE
COO, FM Sales	B3	N/A

REPORTS TO (DIRECT)	REPORTS TO (DIRECT) (GENERIC ROLE)
COO, Financial Markets	
REPORTS TO (INDIRECT)	**REPORTS TO (INDIRECT) (GENERIC ROLE)**
n/a	Global Head, FM Sales
DIRECT REPORTS	**INDIRECT REPORTS**
FM COO Sales team	n/a

JOB PURPOSE

- Ensure robust supervision and control around front-office activities, particularly A&S.
- Ensure robust supervision and management of costs and investments.
- Ensure integration of regulatory change into sales.
- Drive continuous improvements in delivering the cost, client performance and intelligence agenda.
- Drive continuous improvements in the efficiency of sales processes, both operational and organisational.
- Drive process standardisation and best practise across FM sales.

KEY RESPONSIBILITIES

- Define and deliver the agenda to systematically improve client performance/ intelligence, efficiency and control.
- Work in collaboration with OCC, CF, TB and FM products to build effective cross-product cooperation in sales.
- Build and continuously strengthen a culture of risk awareness and proactive resolution across FM sales.
- Build and continuously strengthen processes for tracking client performance and building client intelligence.
- Build and continuously strengthen processes for managing the sales pipeline and revenue forecast.
- Use client performance and intelligence to guide effective resource allocation in conjunction with sales.
- Support the execution of sales strategies with sales.
- Work in collaboration with credit and OCC to agree target clients with respect to A&S.
- Manage the deployment of new regulation to the sales teams.
- Manage communications to FM sales.
- Manage FM sales BAU cost to budget.
- Manage FM sales investment portfolio to budget.
- Manage senior stakeholders in sales and infrastructure functions.
- Manage people development, performance, compensation within team.

Role description continued.

<table>
<tr><th>KEY RELATIONSHIPS</th><th>FOR</th></tr>
<tr><td>• FM PGC chairs and FM PGC secretaries
• FMMG and their direct/indirect reports.
• FMSM.
• COO, OCC.
• Head, TCRM.</td><td>• Overall sales performance.
• Overall operational excellence.
• Overall strength and rigour of the control environment.</td></tr>
<tr><th colspan="2">KEY MEASURABLES</th></tr>
<tr><td colspan="2">• Delivery of both BAU and investment costs to budget.
• Strategic management and positioning of costs for future sustainable growth.
• Improved control environment, observable through audit results, operational losses and control metrics.
• Improved operational efficiency, observable through C&A and other control metrics.
• Improved client performance tracking and client intelligence.
• Client income.</td></tr>
<tr><th colspan="2">REQUIREMENTS</th></tr>
<tr><td colspan="2">• A high-class degree from a top international university.
• Strong interpersonal skills and comfortable operating in a matrix.
• Strong communication skills: oral, written and presentation.
• Is fully conversant with the stakeholders and considered a credible business partner.
• Strong analytical skills and the ability to make sound decisions in a commercial context.
• Strong operational risk and control skills and in particular detailed knowledge of appropriateness and suitability requirements and processes.
• Can demonstrate courage and creativity in a challenging environment.
• Has a strategic mindset with the ability to see beyond the symptoms and into the root of the problem.
• Broad knowledge of financial markets, with at least seven years' experience with sales.
• Advanced technical skills with desktop tools (such as Excel).
• Technology experience both in terms of strategic vision setting and in terms of hard skills.
• Has a strong track record of building performance management and client intelligence capability.
• Has successfully delivered complex projects with tenor greater than six months and budget >$2m.
• Has successfully delivered major projects adopting regulatory reform.
• Has managed $10m+ budget per annum.
• Has managed a multi-location/time-zone team.
• Is multicultural.</td></tr>
</table>

"Career mobility within business management is a challenge. A centralised model has some advantages for career mobility, but fails to address the key requirements for being an effective COO and therefore where else might they be sourced within a company. I strongly believe that there are many people with a sound appreciation of governance and risk and control agendas who might add considerable value in a COO role, not just from within the current business or business management function. But do these other functions see the COO role as their calling? Will the leadership team in charge of such appointments think laterally and consider talent across the whole firm. Are they prepared to take risks on people, or will they stick to hiring from within the function?"

GLOBAL COO, GEOGRAPHIES, GLOBAL WHOLESALE BANK

Career progression of the COO

MD Tier One
(global markets COO)

MD Tier Two
(divisional product COO, e.g., FI or equities)

MD Tier Three
(global product COO)

Director
(regional product COO)

VP
(business manager entrant)

AVP
(business management analyst)

The route to becoming a COO – an analysis of 50 MD COO's within markets, based in New York or London

Education, the bedrock of credibility?

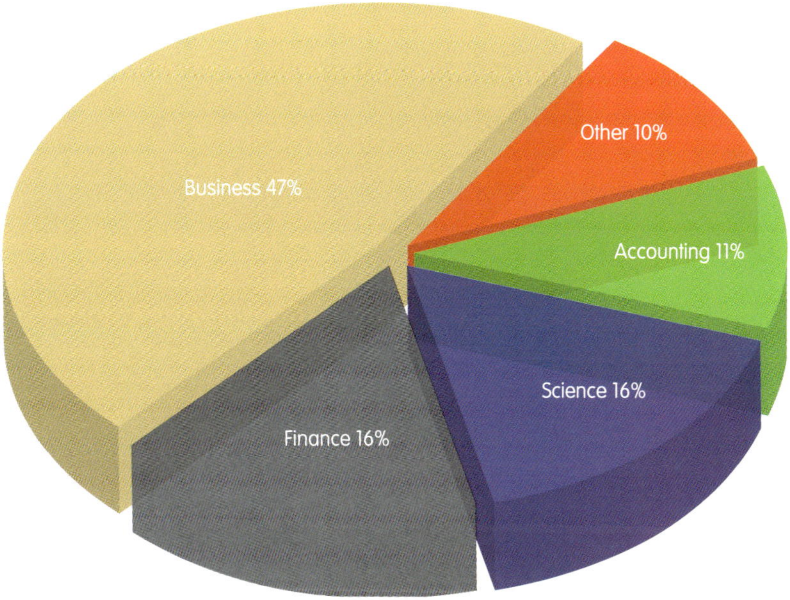

Internationally diverse? 80% of COOs based in the U.K. or the U.S. are British or American.

71% were university graduates. Of this, 50% gained a BA degree, 31% a BSc and 19% a master's.

42% of these graduates went on to do a further professional qualification after completing their degree, of which, half of these were in accountancy.

Research completed by Armstrong Wolfe, October 2016

The route to becoming a COO

Career

25% of the sample group of COOs had previous experience of working for a management consulting company.

60% of COOs previously worked in the infrastructure, e.g., middle office, product control, risk management or audit.

On average, it takes 20 years to be appointed managing director, 14 years to director and 10 years to VP.

24% of COOs also hold another role at the same time.

The average MD COO has worked for 4 employers, with 11% working for 5 or more, in a career spanning over 25 years.

Only 50% of COOs have held 3 or more roles within the same organisation within their career, with 27% holding over 5 roles.

The average term of service in their present role for the COOs surveyed is 2.5 to 3 years.

Excluding previous career experience in professional services, only 15% had a meaningful career outside financial services, before embarking on their banking career.

Research completed by Armstrong Wolfe, October 2016

Attributes COOs 'strongly believe' were needed for their career development

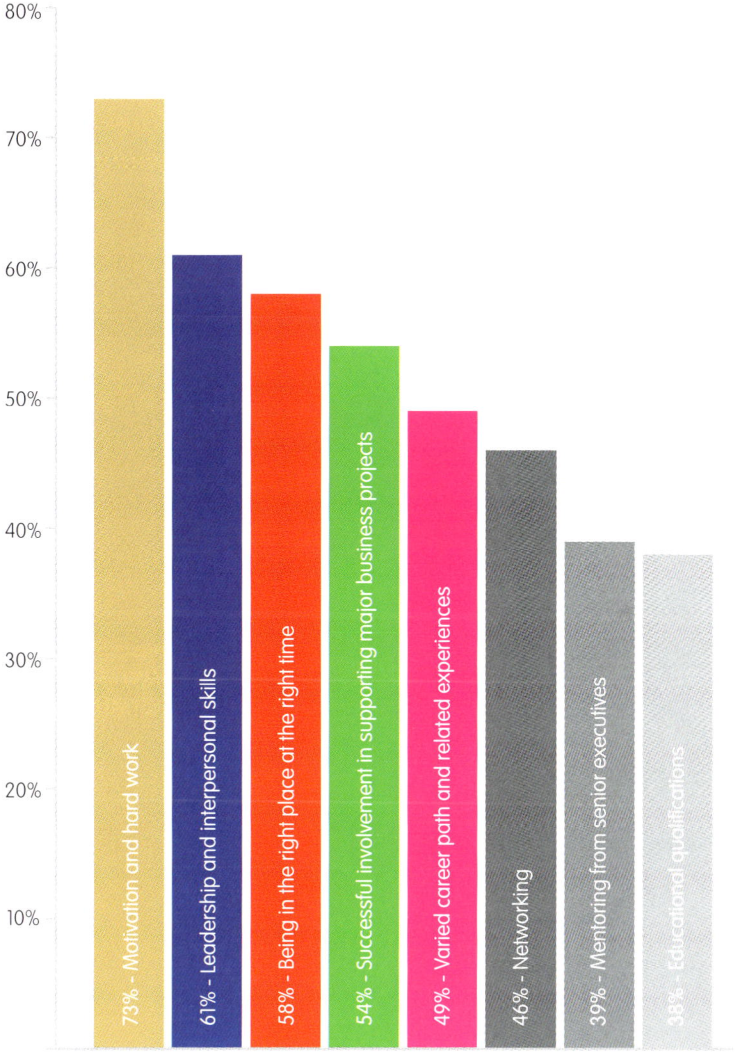

Research completed by Armstrong Wolfe, October 2016

"When hiring and developing talent within the COO and business management function, it is important to think about what problem you are trying to solve. Banks tend to look for talent within the existing COO team, not externally. That might be okay in a product COO role; an individual might have the required knowledge of key products, but it does not necessarily mean they have broad management experience or an appreciation of the overall management agenda and priorities across the whole firm. These are the areas to focus on when looking to hire the right person – fit for role, not for purpose."

GLOBAL COO, GEOGRAPHIES, GLOBAL WHOLESALE BANK

Behavioural attributes of the COO

Executing	Influencing	Relationship building	Strategic thinking
People with dominant executing themes know how to 'make things happen'.	People with dominant influencing themes know how to take charge, speak up, and make sure the team is heard.	People with dominant relationship building themes have the ability to build strong relationships that can hold a team together and make the team greater than the sum of its parts.	People with dominant strategic thinking themes help teams consider what could be. They absorb and analyse information that can inform better decisions.
Achiever Arranger Belief Consistency Deliberative Discipline Focus Responsibility Restorative	Activator Command Communication Competition Maximiser Self-Assurance Significance Woo	Adaptability Connectedness Developer Empathy Harmony Includer Individualisation Positivity Relater	Analytical Context Futuristic Ideation Input Intellection Learner Strategic

Research completed by Armstrong Wolfe, October 2016

Talent acquisition – VP entry

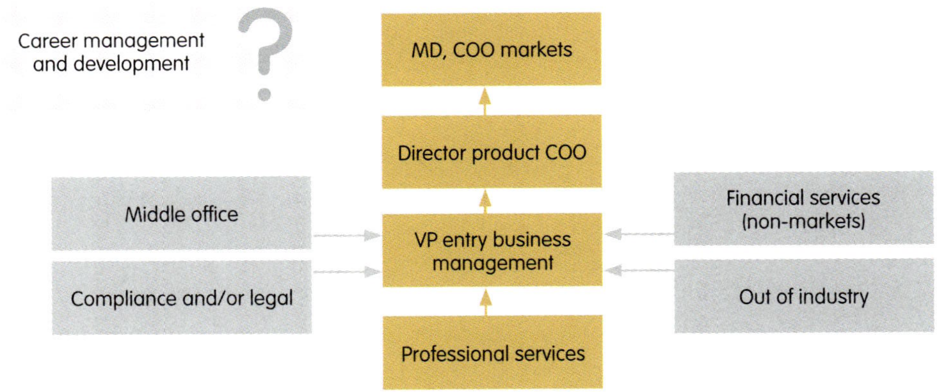

NBC UNIVERSAL
THE JAY
SHARP
AQUOS
CHAMPS
ONE WAY
Van Wagner
CHAMPS
SPORTS
AMSTERDAM
SEPHORA

RICOH
100% ECO-POWERED BILLBOARD
PRINT • COPY • SCAN • SOLUTIONS
ricoh-eco.com
CHASE
BUSES ONLY
7AM - 10 AM
4 PM - 7 PM
MON thru FRI
7AM-7PM
NEW VICTORY
NEW VICTORY
NEW VICTORY
Walgreens

"My argument is that women in the COO community add equal or greater value in the COO role than men, so more should be done to promote and retain female COOs."

WOMEN IN THE COO COMMUNITY

The commercial case for equality-plus representation

I have always felt that women make more effective COOs than men but have been hesitant to state this openly, fearing that my views on commonly associated behavioural skills such as influence, empathy, collaboration, integrity and so on would be seen as clichéd or stereotypical. I also struggled to know how best to express my feeling that women also make for a highly effective number two, supporting a principal executive (whether that principal is a man or a woman). Women seem frequently to demonstrate a selfless commitment to a common and overriding goal and this, of course, is a key attribute for a COO.

I have researched this matter extensively and have heard my suppositions tested with hundreds – if not thousands – of references to the capabilities of women, sometimes in the form of passing comments and at other times as exact and targeted observations or official references. The conclusion I have reached is that there is a straightforward commercial need for women to be found in the COO community in equal, perhaps even in greater, numbers than men.

Any analysis of this subject, however, must be carried out in the context of the banking COO specifically, as this can differ substantially from the same position elsewhere. Even within the banking sector, the role and responsibilities of the COO can vary due to the proliferation and liberal distribution of the COO title in recent years. The execution of the COO's job can be very different within the front office itself, let alone from the same role by title in the infrastructure (although some of the workload may be comparable). As one infrastructure COO put it:

> *"There are two types of COOs in the front office. There are those with a risk, finance, operations or product control background. Here their role tends to be aligned to their heritage, such as risk management, expense management, regulatory oriented or project focused, and then there is the minority where you really are the right-hand man or women of the CEO. … The career tracking is different and they need to think more consciously about the skill-set they have. … I think the issue around low numbers of women in these roles starts at the point of recruitment at the more junior levels, making sure there is a more defined career path and support."*

My research covered all COO roles, in a variety of regions and functions. The results showed that in all areas, there was a constant challenge to demonstrate equality – and sometimes even basic representation – at the leadership table. During my research I read many sources. One in particular is worthy of mention here: a *Harvard Business Review* paper titled 'Are Women Better Leaders than Men?' (Jack Zenger and Joseph Folkman, 2012.). This is not specific to the COO, but many of the competencies it assesses are found within any COO role. This paper inspired several of the questions I put to female COOs in my own research, all linked to the central question, "Do women make better COOs than men, and if so, why?"

One of my contacts, who has held executive positions in various functions and disciplines within banking and who has more recently moved into a COO role supporting a group CFO, summarised her thoughts on this matter:

> *"I have seen very good male and female COOs and poor male and female COOs. I don't agree therefore that women have innate competencies that make them better in this role. However, I do agree that there are fewer female front-office COOs than there could be, and that's largely a function of the ratio imbalance of men to women in the front office generally. It also depends on the role. If it is [seen as] a stepping stone in a front-office context, then the female (or any) COO will need to have a demonstrable revenue track record – and here specifically this group of women is much smaller."*

It was with this initial feedback that I approached a number of female executive COOs for their thoughts.

Question 1

Do you believe that women make better COOs than men?

I deliberately began with a yes or no question, although I expected anything but simplistic answers. In truth, the question is not so much whether women make better COOs, but rather why they do (or don't) and why they might be perceived as a better fit than men. In such a complex role, assessing the common responsibilities of the COO would help determine the answer.

Common themes are the nature and demands of the role. This is a full-on, often 24/7, job, which can make it difficult for women with family commitments. I know that many people will disagree, claiming that this factor is no longer relevant, but a reasonable percentage of the women asked raised this point. Some women have a partner whose own commitments allow her to be at the end of the phone to deal with issues as they arise, but this is not always the case.

A few women suggested that there are still remnants of old-fashioned attitudes that work against women. One commented: "Many COO-to-manager relationships have been cemented in social interaction in the bar, [but] I can hardly see myself popping my head around the corner of my boss's office saying 'shall we grab a beer tonight to cover a few points?'" Such attitudes can challenge equal opportunities. Demands of the role such as long hours are being addressed by policy and cultural change, but in reality most people accept that being a COO means allowing others constant access to you. One can only hope that the office-bar dynamic is a legacy of the past that will fade with the rise of a new managerial generation.

It is the behavioural differences between men and women that really strengthen the case for women making better COOs. While some of the women interviewed gave a straight 'yes' or 'no' answer to the question, most carved out a diplomatic path, which in itself suggests that women may be better suited than men to such a role:

> *"Top-level COOs have tended to be male and have been selected for the role based on previous roles of being No. 1/head of a front office/sales-type division rather than coming through the ranks in a more business manager/strategy-type role. In this observation, I would say that the people selected have had the strategy and leadership strengths analogous to the No. 1 (e.g., the CEO), but not the No. 2 (COO) attention to detail/follow-through/multi-tasking skills that may, at face value, be a more generic female trait.*
> *By the same token I would say that if you see the CEO/COO balance to be that the former sets the agenda and the latter executes the agenda, then the COO would also require the more strategic/killer instinct to effectively cascade down and drive forward the agenda. I wonder therefore if it's the next level down that … tends to capture the more stereotyped 'female' trait people."*
>
> GLOBAL COO, CLEARING SERVICES

> *"I think it depends upon the individual. No two COO roles are the same, and therefore, the skill-*

set needed varies. I think there needs to be more gender balance in the COO community. It is difficult for a woman to excel in this field when the definitions of success often still link back to old-fashioned traditionally male traits such as working long hours, networking in the bar etc. rather than what is actually delivered."

COO TO CHIEF CONTROL OFFICER

"I think women make better COOs because the job of the COO is never done and women don't naturally do the least they can get away with – they are naturally diligent and seek to please their bosses – I am of course generalising to make a point, for impact."

EMEA COO, MARKETS

"No. I think this is not a gender question, but a skill question. In my experience as a COO and employing junior to senior members of a COO team, I have found both men and women to be equally capable and equally incapable of performing as a high-functioning COO. The only place … where perhaps you could argue that gender plays a part is in the "softer" and sometimes necessary skills that come with parts of some COO roles. Some examples include

having that innate intuition or pulse of the employees, or, in finance, which is still heavily male dominated, be a natural point person."

GLOBAL COO, DISTRIBUTION

"More often than not women are better at multi-tasking, they are more organised and think beyond just themselves, by considering the potential impact that something can have on others and the broader community as well. Women are also intuitively more practical, and so will consider the practicalities of implementing a process or control as well as focusing on the end result. All these qualities or skills are very relevant for a COO and can often differentiate between a successful COO, who progresses and adds value to organisation, versus someone who enjoys the title but is unable to accomplish what is required.

Someone once said to me that a successful COO is someone that is comfortable and also happy to be the No. 2. … I think women often feel comfortable in that position [while] men will often struggle – perhaps it is an ego thing, or a sense of over-confidence that kicks in."

CHIEF OF STAFF TO GLOBAL HEAD OF EQUITIES

Question 2

Other than well-established issues such as insufficient support for those with families, shortcomings in equitable promotion and pay, etc., what factors unique to the role of the COO inhibit career progression for women?

It was universally acknowledged that the challenge for women to gain equal representation in opportunity and career advancement was no different in this role than in any other in banking. "I do not think that any of the issues are specific to COO roles", commented one. All the principal banks are operating and working on their equality agenda, albeit at different paces and with varying results. "We will have to therefore work on both sides, reducing the costs through flexible work arrangement and increasing the benefits through genuine development plans that make career progression a reality."

However, my argument is that women in the COO community add equal or greater value in the COO role than men, so more should be done to promote and retain female COOs. The question should therefore be, "What can be done over and above what is already being done?"

Although I could find no reliable data to confirm it, there do seem to be more women than men in visible leadership positions within a COO role. This may be because the COO role "offers the ability to do things like work flexibly but still be in a front office environment", as one woman questioned suggested. My own research suggests that 25–30 per cent of banking COOs are women, but this of course does not present the full picture of female leadership in banking. For that you need to consider the ratio of men to women as business heads alongside the ratios within the COO community.

Conversations on this subject were diverse, and opinions and proposed solutions varied. Evidence that establishing equal, or near-equal, female representation at COO level pays commercial dividends would help this cause, but the ambiguous nature of the COO role makes this a qualitative and not a quantitative assessment and, thus, hard to prove:

> *"The fact is that there are not enough mid-level female managers in banking overall. Statistics show that whilst women make up 50 per cent or more of the junior positions, the proportion of women decreases at each level as we move up the hierarchy. Women are exiting at higher rates than men, and they are being hired at a lower rate. For women the costs of working in the financial industry still seem to outweigh the benefits; as a result they leave the industry."*
>
> GLOBAL COO, UK WHOLESALE BANK

> *"I don't necessarily think there is anything explicit that is lacking to enable more women to take on the roles of COO. Unfortunately, I think the same issues that are discussed in all organisations around female leadership, progression, unconscious bias, networking, political savvy all ring true, and organisations can only do so much to change those factors both within the organisation but also within women themselves.*

I think for women 'mentoring' is a big factor in terms of developing the skills to step up the ladder. Women need that nod of approval more than men in order to put their head above the parapet. I think this also goes to being in the 'inner circle' to be selected for roles, particularly higher up the chain. The harsh reality is that people like to select people who they know, who they have worked with, who they trust and too often who are like them. For a number of explicit as well as implicit reasons, women tend to both be excluded and exclude themselves from this inner circle."

GLOBAL COO, FUTURES AND OPTIONS

"As the relationship between the business leader and COO needs to be highly effective for it to be of value, often COOs are picked from a pool of people the business leader already knows. As the majority of the front office is male, they will only have a small pool of female candidates to pick from. Even when a female is appointed to a COO role, people will assume it is more administrative in nature than when a male colleague is in a similar role."

GLOBAL COO TO CHIEF CONTROL OFFICER

"I don't see structural problems that hinder women in the COO space particularly. I would say that rather this is one of the areas where you tend to see more senior women because the COO role offers the ability to do things like work flexibly, but still be in a front-office environment. My COO staff is over 30 per cent female at all levels – this is way above the female participation rates in other front-office areas."

EMEA COO, MARKETS

"I think it is an excellent role for a woman and can complement a women's skill-set incredibly well. Perhaps to achieve senior success as a COO, though, a woman needs to be extremely driven (which can often be the case) – but also be prepared to push very hard to take things forward. Not afraid to deal with some extremely tough situations. … Let's not forget that a COO is not a glamorous role. It requires quick thinking and a very self-assertive attitude to get things done. … I do think that this aspect of the role can be daunting to anyone, and maybe more so to a woman in a very male environment – so a successful female COO will need to be confident to work through all aspects of the role with determination and grit. They might need

to work harder than their equivalent male – but actually I also think it's about working smarter."

CHIEF OF STAFF TO GLOBAL HEAD OF EQUITIES

Question 3

What could be done specifically within the COO and business management community to address the shortage of low female representation at the mid to senior level of this community?

This question dovetails with Question 2, but interestingly the answers were more direct and pointed. Those interviewed seemed to understand that behavioural development and building confidence in female COOs would be a good start in establishing a stable of talent for the future: "Resilience is key; whatever we can do to help women build this reliance will make a difference."

Aligned to this is a need to improve the perception, understanding and awareness of the COO role at an early stage in someone's career. Such steps are necessary in order to attract the best men and women into this community. They demand a path for advancement within the business management community and managers willing to invest in their staff's development. "If they don't have a decent line manager, a sponsor or structure around them that can nurture, provide support and answer important questions, how can you expect someone to be successful?" This is particularly true of women who want both a successful career and a family.

Developing an effective and well-supported return-to-work policy for women who have taken time out for family, married to a strong culture at all levels of embracing such choices, will in time help to address the issue of inequality in female representation in the

COO community. I believe it is easy to accommodate a workplace/home working structure and to allow opportunities for job sharing. In addition, women with years of previous and varied experience can often be welcomed back into a business management function, allowing them to rapidly refamiliarise themselves with the market. The return on this investment, commitment and cooperation will be in establishing a more representative and effective business management function. This is more relevant today than ever, especially when good conduct, behaviour and culture are at the forefront of any CEO's and COO's agenda:

> *"I don't think there is anything different for the COO space than there is for the rest of the financial industry. A career in the financial industry is hard and can be exhausting in the long run, both for men and for women. We need to make sure the benefits are as attractive for women as they are for men."*
>
> GLOBAL COO, UK WHOLESALE BANK

> *"I don't think someone in a mid- to senior-level COO role within a firm is necessarily the person who becomes the company COO. Perhaps this leads to a gap in certain types of leadership skills, strategy-based skills more commonly needed in the CEO No. 2 role. By the same token the CEO No. 2 can lack the more detail-driven competencies acquired through non-P&L-generating functions.*

Perhaps some networking forums around both the skill gap closing and the education of the space may help to close the gender gap. Certainly, I think the COO space at any level is one that people fall into rather than actively aspire to, simply through lack of understanding or awareness of the space."

GLOBAL COO, FUTURES AND OPTIONS

"Remove the need for so much self-promotion from the promotion process. Often people who talk about delivery and who actively network are promoted, as they are deemed to have 'presence and gravitas'. This disadvantages women who generally (but not exclusively) prefer to be judged on their work ethic and what they have delivered and will actively try not to 'brag'."

GLOBAL COO, CONTROL AND CONDUCT

"There is not one magic answer, but I do think that there is some key, consistent practises that can move us towards one day seeing more woman at the mid to senior level. First off, though, why do women derail from what looks like a promising career path? … I think women (in finance) in COO roles (just like other roles) tend to not have the network and informal mentoring that

is needed. Firms need to continue to identify the high potential (female) talent early on and embrace them, help them build their network, give them senior sponsors. Senior women also need to view it as their responsibility to be a voice to support these women as well. At the same time middle (male) management needs to be trained on unconscious bias behaviour."

GLOBAL COO, FIXED INCOME

"Often I think that juniors to mid-level females become disillusioned as they start to progress if they don't have a decent line manager, a sponsor or structure around them that can nurture, provide support and answer important questions around how you be successful in your career as a woman and also start a family. A lack of support at this stage can encourage females to either move out of the industry or when they do start a family, decide that they can't return to work. …

Females have a range of different needs when they are at work, but often they need to be encouraged to put themselves forward for roles. A female is often more likely to think that they can't do a bigger role, whereas a guy will think he can do a bigger role, even when he may not be experienced or ready for it. The lack of confidence with the

female can inhibit progression, but can actually quite easily be overcome through support and sponsorship if implemented at the right time in a female's career. …
I have seen so many talented junior females enter the COO/business management community – and if we can do a better job to nurture and support them right from the start and make sure that their line managers are also trained to effectively do the same, then I think that over time we will have better female representation at the more senior level as well."

FORMER GLOBAL COO, EQUITIES

So, is there a commercial argument and moral case for greater female representation in the COO community? Yes. Do women make better COOs than men? Yes. Is this my opinion and that of the majority asked – having surveyed both men and women? Yes.

Naturally, women do not want quotas; they want to be promoted on merit. The challenge for women, especially within the front office, is finding the opportunity to demonstrate they are worthy of such promotion. The issue is threefold:

1 How do you attract the best women into business management, develop and retain them?
2 How do you structure an effective return-to-work programme for those who have taken a career break to start a family?
3 How do you create a platform of equal opportunity and visibility for women in the COO community, especially in the male-dominated front office?

If I were a CEO (or king for a day!), my aim would be at least equal representation of women and men within my COO team – not to fulfil a quota but to maximise commercial performance. I have drafted my speech to my fellow and fictional board members as such:

> *"Let us start with an objective of 35 per cent – at least that is a step in the right direction and one that is achievable if we combine the steely determination of the female COOs and business managers we have already with those who we will identify and nurture for tomorrow, and combine their will and commitment to the task, knowing they have a boss, a management team, their company and the industry's support and recognition to do so. The aim is equal representation as a by-product of individual performance by the women in our COO and leadership team, not equal representation because a quota demands it. By creating a platform of equal opportunity for this group, we will convert this investment into commercial benefit for the company."*

Appendix

Are Women Better Leaders than Men?

By Jack Zenger and Joseph Folkman, March 15th 2012
Reprinted by permission of *Harvard Business Review*

We've all heard the claims, the theories, and the speculation about the ways leadership styles vary between women and men.

Our data comes from 360 evaluations, so what they are tracking is the judgment of a leader's peers, bosses, and direct reports. We ask these individuals to rate each leader's effectiveness overall and also to judge how strong he or she is on the 16 competencies that our 30 years of research shows are most important to overall leadership effectiveness. We ask, for instance, how good a leader is at taking the initiative, developing others, inspiring and motivating, and pursuing their own development.

Our latest survey of 7,280 leaders, which our organization evaluated in 2011, reproduce some seemingly eternal truths about men and women leaders in the workplace but also holds some surprises. Our dataset was generated from leaders in some of the most successful and progressive organizations in the world both public and private, government and commercial, domestic and international.

In the confirmation category is our first finding: the majority of leaders (64%) are still men. And the higher the level, the more men there are: In this group, 78% of top managers were men, 67% at the next level down (that is, senior executives reporting directly to the top managers), 60% at the manager level below that.

Similarly, most stereotypes would have us believe that female leaders excel at "nurturing" competencies such as developing others and building relationships, and many might put exhibiting integrity and engaging in self-development in that category as well. And in all four cases our data concurred — women did score higher than men.

But the women's advantages were not at all confined to traditionally women's strengths. In fact at every level, more women were rated by their peers, their bosses, their direct reports, and their other associates as better overall leaders than their male counterparts — and the higher the level, the wider that gap grows.

Specifically, at all levels, women are rated higher in fully 12 of the 16 competencies that go into outstanding leadership. And two of the traits where women outscored men to the highest degree — taking initiative and driving for results — have long been thought of as particularly male strengths. As it happened, men outscored women significantly on only one management competence in this survey — the ability to develop a strategic perspective.

So what should we conclude from these data? Why are we not engaging and fully employing these exemplary women leaders? Yes, blatant discrimination is a potential explanation. If not actual than certainly perceptual. When we shared our findings with a group of women outside this particular survey and asked them to suggest why they thought their colleagues had been rated so highly on taking initiative and self-development, their answers pointed to the still-tenuous position they feel themselves to be in the workplace:

"We need to work harder than men to prove ourselves."

"We feel the constant pressure to never make a mistake and to continually prove our value to the organization."

That is, anecdotally, at least, the women we queried don't feel their appointments are safe. They're afraid to rest on their laurels. Feeling the need (often keenly) to take initiative, they are more highly motivated to take feedback to heart.

The irony is that these are fundamental behaviours that drive the success of every leader, whether woman or man.

Why are women viewed as less strategic? This is an easier question to answer. Top leaders always score significantly higher in this competency; since more top leaders are men, men still score higher here in the aggregate.

But when we measure only men and women in top management on strategic perspective, their relative scores are the same.

What should leaders and managers do with these findings? Here are our thoughts.

As leaders in organisations look hard to find the talent they need to achieve exceptional results, they ought to be aware that many women have impressive leadership skills. Our research shows these leadership skills are strongly correlated to organizational success factors such as retaining talent, customer satisfaction, employee engagement, and profitability.

As to the constant state of unease we hear women leaders express — clearly, chauvinism or discrimination is an enigma that organisations (and the business culture) should work hard to prevent. However, that said, think of the benefits every leader in every organization would gain from a mind-set that they simply can't afford to make a mistake. Paranoia or extreme risk aversion is clearly detrimental to a rising career. But in today's economic climate, every leader, male or female, would do well to avoid becoming complacent.

"We should not discount the common behavioural traits so often found in military personnel and the benefits they can bring to a commercial organisation."

FROM THE ACADEMIES OF SANDHURST AND WEST POINT TO THE OFFICE OF THE COO

The transfer of military leadership experience into banking

It is not purely the loyalty and romanticism linked to being ex-military myself that frames my thoughts on why ex-servicemen and -women make great COOs. However, having been a soldier certainly helps me understand why they do, and, combined with more than 20 years of executive search experience, this enables me to find those leaving the military a place in the banking sector well suited to their skills and interests.

Since leaving the army in 1995, I have worked almost exclusively within recruitment for the financial services sector, specifically within financial markets and investment banking. I have found career opportunities for perhaps more than a hundred soldiers, sailors and pilots in this time. These young men and women had been pre-selected, then trained at one of the leadership academies, further trained in their specialist disciplines and then tested on operational tours, mostly in the Middle East. They had left the military by their own choice, and while many hiring managers questioned why they would want to exchange the dynamic and challenging world of the military for a desk, a computer and a window overlooking Canary Wharf, they had made this decision in good faith and were set on using what they had learned in the forces to forge a worthwhile career in the civilian world.

Initially my searches were based on a generic appreciation of the inherent skill-set of all ex-officers, across all services: leadership, tenacity, integrity, articulateness and intellect. It was easy to find entry-level roles for such men and women, and I knew that if their line manager valued them and could see the potential that I saw, it would not be long before these new recruits into banking would catch up with – and possibly even pass – their peers on the career ladder. However, it soon became clear that I needed to fine-tune my approach. The general behavioural attributes I credit to ex-servicemen and -women are very important, but I realised that the technical skill-sets acquired in the military could be matched in banking with a greater level of understanding and accuracy.

Many banks now have their own military programmes, hiring directly from the services. In the U.S. there is a far more open corporate effort and commitment to this than there is in the U.K.(JPMorgan and Bank of America are two of the most active in this area). This is mainly because there is a greater sense of social responsibility towards veterans in the U.S., and this combines with a recognition that, if hired, trained and positioned correctly, this talent pool of lateral hires could add real value to the industry. However, programmes do exist in the U.K., too. Barclays is at the forefront of this effort, with a notably broad-based recruiting platform that draws from both officer and non-officer ranks (most recruiting strategies for banking focus on graduates, thus confining themselves largely to officers).

Broadly speaking, hiring managers tend to see ex-military applicants as part of one large, equally qualified talent pool. In most cases it is the presentation, impact and personality of the individual that determines his or her success at interview. However, this overlooks the great diversity of skills members of this pool have to offer. Progress through the Sandhurst leadership pipeline suggests they are all on the same footing, but when they leave to follow their individual career in the military, what they do, how they are trained and the skill-sets they develop are very different from one another.

An engineering officer, for example, builds credibility in project management and addressing technical challenges, such as building a bridge, dismantling an airfield, dealing with IODs, and so on. Their leadership skills are built on managing similarly technically minded individuals in a project cycle of military demands. An Infantry officer are different. Their leadership skills are more traditional and motivational. Many would say the role of the infantry officer is physically more demanding than that of an engineering officer, drawing on and encouraging a can-do attitude, leading by example and developing strong relationship and even sales skills. Infantry officers might lack the eye for detail that engineering officers posses, but they offer instead a robust approach to getting things done. It is no surprise, therefore, to find many ex-engineering officers in consulting, project management or in an operations environment. Infantry officers have moved successfully into sales or business management and the roles of COO, CAO or CoS. However, it is often the case that these men and women have steered their career in these directions themselves, through self-management and hard work, rather than having been positioned on the right path at the beginning of their transition from the military to banking.

Such comments are, of course, generalisations, but they highlight an important lesson: when hiring from the military, it is important to really understand the individual, their talents and their experience. Despite this, we should not discount the common behavioural traits so often found in military personnel and the benefits they can bring to a commercial organisation. In my opinion, one of the most valuable of these characteristics is a strong sense of purpose. The British writer Roderic Yapp investigates this in his article 'The real reason the military works':

"It is written into our doctrine – our standard way of doing things. Every mission is required to have what is called 'a unifying purpose'. A mission statement must include the phrase 'in order to'…

- *It is our mission to recapture this vessel in order to secure the safe release of the hostages.*
- *It is our mission to conduct a patrol of the local area in order to reassure the local population.*
- *It is our mission to provide a block to the south of Musa-Qala in order to prevent enemy reinforcements from reaching the town.*

When you are taught how to write orders, you are taught that soldiers and marines need a purpose – a reason to do what you ask of them.

They're no different from anyone else in that respect, they need to know why they are doing something – they don't just do it because someone tells them to. They don't do it because they are just following orders. When people simply follow orders, it usually leads to bad things happening because they don't stop to think if it is the right thing to do.

Having a purpose is vital, both at an individual and at a team level. The military make sure that they provide a purpose in every mission statement – it wouldn't be a mission statement without an 'in order to'. This approach has been standardised across NATO because it is universal – it crosses cultural boundaries addressing the need we all have for a purpose behind our actions."

This sense of purpose is instilled in all those who enter military service and it informs everything they do, underpinning their actions and framing their attitude. This readily translates into responding to orders and getting things done, being objective and target driven. It often relies on effective management, but even here most ex-military can operate effectively in a leadership void – they are trained to step up a rank at any given time.

Purpose is married to service and integrity (relevant in the financial sector, which grapples with the conduct agenda). It also goes hand in hand with an ability to work within ambiguity and to carve out a route to delivery. These are also attributes demonstrated by the best COOs and business managers. However, my conclusion that the COO role is perfectly aligned to the skills, personality and experiences of those leaving the military needed to be tested. This led me to ask a series of questions to those formerly in the armed services and now in senior positions in the financial services sector. The answers make interesting reading.

What is it that makes the likelihood of success high when banks hire from the military?

> *"A willingness to learn and take direction – the military is a constant training laboratory to create generalists and generals. Loyalty – they have been in the mud when the chips were down and did not lose their nerve. [They] have absorbed some tough 'debriefs', willing to be a part of, and have, tough conversations – these are often the conversations that really matter."*
>
> FORMER US MARINE CORPS FIGHTER PILOT AND TOP GUN INSTRUCTOR

"I believe that ex-officers have the skills required and have an attitude that is less 'gen x' – i.e., the world does not revolve around me – and that is extremely helpful dealing with senior folk. The skills that coming from the captain and above ranks are … the ability to challenge respectfully but firmly when in possession of facts. Challenge, and the ability to deal with rejected challenge, is a core skill required but not often appreciated in the roles of COO, etc.

Additionally, drive and passion come from the military background. You know that Sandhurst has put someone through the stress tests and they have survived and will bring the same to bear to get the task done irrespective of the personal inconvenience."

FORMER BRITISH ARMY CAPTAIN, NOW SENIOR EXECUTIVE WITHIN IB OPERATIONS

"A cliché, but there is a proven track record of delivery under (in some instances) incredibly testing circumstances. We react well to pressure. Ex-service officers have the ability to synthesise and simplify complex problems, break them into their constituent parts in order to find and execute solutions. They also come to the industry, any industry, with no historic baggage,

no preconceptions and a questioning attitude. Finally, the majority of them have honed their practical leadership skills in a testing environment, not from a book. This clearly has a knock-on effect on the quality and use of our softer skills."

FORMER INFANTRY OFFICER, BRITISH ARMY, WHO HAS MANAGED VARIOUS SENIOR BANKING OPERATIONS, CAO AND COO ROLES POST SERVICE

"The officer is somewhat of a known quantity. Officers join companies (financial institutions) with a large management tick by their name considering: equipment (systems and change), people (FTE, including offshoring, depth charting and flight risk), risk (intelligent preparation of the battle field), control/compliance (rules of engagement, orders, LOE, etc.) and regulation (laws of armed conflict, legitimacy versus legality). But perhaps most importantly, they understand and can depict tactical versus strategic planning and actions. This broad exposure marks each individual out from a pack."

FORMER BRITISH ARMY CAPTAIN, WHO HAS SUBSEQUENTLY HELD POSITIONS IN INVESTMENT BANKING AND INSURANCE IN ASIA AND EUROPE

"There are so many variables depending on the circumstances of both the candidate and client.

It is, therefore, impossible to prescribe a formula for success. However, if I had to boil it down to three factors, I'd suggest:

Fit (arguably the most critical factor):

- *All parties need to understand how they can maximise the capacity, tap leadership potential and adjust communication styles where required.*
- *Prior to joining, possibly even before accepting the offer, there should be a one- to two-day period of familiarisation and role introduction; try before you buy.*
- *Understanding the power of a strong internal network; without this, success is unlikely and advancement will be very challenging.*

Full understanding of the hiring manager's expectations:

- *Specific initial deliverables. Of course there will be some ambiguity, but some early defined success can give a good initial boost to profile and confidence.*
- *Complete tasks. It sounds obvious but banking is built on numbers and closing issues. Understanding and driving performance metrics/MI is part of the game. Be a finisher!*
- *House style (dos/don'ts). Potentially a*

minefield if one misunderstands or makes assumptions. The uniformed world is clearly badged and identified, hierarchies are easy to spot and navigate; in the commercial world, this needs careful consideration. It can be hard to break into and gain trust.

• Frequent feedback sessions for first three to four months. Need to be open, frank and honest.

Personal support plan tailored to the level of the role. Could include but not limited to:

• Dedicated peer to help adjust to internal processes for first four to six months.

• Non-line manager mentor to provide guidance and a sounding board for ideas.

• Exposure to areas outside immediate role to broaden network, improve understanding and raise awareness."

FORMER WING COMMANDER AND CHIEF OF STAFF TO THE HEAD OF THE RAF, WHO HAS SUBSEQUENTLY ESTABLISHED A SUCCESSFUL CAREER IN CONTROL, CONDUCT AND FRONT OFFICE BUSINESS MANAGEMENT WITHIN INVESTMENT BANKING

I then sought to validate my thoughts that skills are matched, but not well matched, and that some fine-tuning would benefit the individual and the employer.

I returned to my network and gathered further opinions. Those below are drawn from the three services: navy, army and air force.

These anonymous quotes represent the opinions of those who left as lieutenants through to brigadiers, from infantry to signals officers, from submariners to pilots and men and women that served, all leaving to pursue careers in the financial services sector.

Do you feel the exact skills and experiences are well matched at the point of hiring, or are you more likely to find your niche, plough your own furrow, through trial and error once established?

> *"Both. The experiences and skills are relevant and matter. Yet you build your own reputation by demonstrating your ability to deliver. Remember – a reputation is a terrible thing to waste."*

> *"I do not think skills will be an exact match on hiring – different TLAs for a start. But intelligence and application allow the new joiner to thrive fast and different roles exist as they do in the military, so finding the furrow is likely to take time."*

> *"I think the latter. … Ex-service officers can turn their hand to just about anything. We all leverage the same skill-set – communication, organisation, leadership, structure – but we utilise them in different fields, e.g., project management, risk management or CoS/COO roles. Ultimately this proves the value of our*

versatility and the ability of the employer to parachute us into any difficult situation which requires resolution."

"I strongly believe the skills are very well matched. I feel officers do, however, make a bad job of marketing themselves effectively. I have fallen into a common group where I have tried to market myself as a jack of all trades. I think employers have a grasp for the qualities synonymous with an officer, but this doesn't mean that an officer can't drill down to the minutiae in order to get that first role, to specialise and command a niche. This is where going for coffee, listening to good recruiters and applying some lateral thought come in."

"I agree … that those from technical corps background are more likely to be suited to programme management or technical consulting roles. Age and seniority, though, can be significant factors in determining how well matched the candidate will be in the short term:

- *For those who would have been considered top 10 per cent officers, the change of profile can be very difficult. However, slightly easier to manage in technical roles (programme management/IT, etc.) where transferable skills map more directly.*

- *For top third, it is easier to adjust subject to personal goals and circumstances; SO2 feels like an experience sweet spot here.*
- *For middle of the road, they are easier to manage, are less frustrated and, put simply, are just grateful to have a job that covers school fees.*
- *For junior officers, it's a world of opportunity, and irrespective of experience, if they have the right fit, they can achieve almost anything. They have time on their side and can move laterally with little penalty or risk.*
- *Regrettably, more senior officers (SO1 and above) can often struggle to adjust to the relatively low levels of early responsibility and – dare I say it – status.*

Finding one's 'niche' is probably more due to luck than proactive planning. Opportunities will emerge as one's network grows and reputation builds. However, to paraphrase, 'the more one practises, i.e. exposed to senior business leaders, the luckier one becomes…' Consequently, if the initial entry role doesn't quite fit, then cut your losses early; get out there, be seen and make your own luck… Trial and error can work, but only for so long. The window of opportunity probably closes with two to three years. A significant change of direction at this point is risky and needs to be considered very carefully."

'Finding one's niche', getting better advice, guidance and insight – all aspects that most ex-military personnel say would have helped them enter banking in a role well suited to their skills and experiences. I further investigated this with the following question.

If you could rewind to your own hiring process, what would you have done differently in managing your own entry into banking?

"My entry was odd, but I did have a degree in banking and finance so had a head start. I would also recommend before people retire that they read the FT and the Economist so they get a flavour of the lingo."

"I would definitely be more self-aware of the power of brand and self-publicity. The majority of ex-service officers are not good at self-promoting or talking about their time in uniform. We are usually too modest to talk about the tougher times that have defined who we are and how we do our business, and additionally do not want to be seen to be 'swinging the lantern' or becoming the ex-military bore."

"Maybe ask for more money – it's difficult to ask for more after you have started. I did make a mistake with Swiss Re. The hiring manager raised warning signs within me about his personality and management style but I chose to plough on. I didn't smell the coffee!"

"I would have invested more time in understanding how the bank actually works:

- *Products, processes, systems, VaR, cost of capital, RWA, balance sheet, trading/banking book, PnL, etc.*
- *Spend time with ops, IT systems, trade capture, reconciliations.*
- *Clients? Who are they and how do they operate. How does the bank service?*
- *More seriously considered if an internal support role (COO/BM) was actually what I wanted to do and if this played to my strengths. With hindsight, I think I would rather have sought a relationship manager position where I could exploit my communication and interpersonal skills.*
- *Decide whether managing a team is important. If so, how important? Often BM roles, especially more junior ones, have limited responsibilities here, and this may frustrate many who are more*

used to shaping a team and developing their staff.

- *Learn Excel. I'm not joking. I defy anyone to succeed without a good understanding of this software and its functionality. If you can't do it, then make sure you have a team member who is an Excel ninja; they will be your best asset when cutting through the data and analysing issues."*

Conversely, on the same subject one client commented:

> *"There needs to be an openness and discussion about the pitfalls of hiring from military – short-term commissions verses longer servers. For instance, I have never seen anyone higher than an army captain be really successful in transition to the financial services, and I have seen some real disasters in hiring majors and colonels. … I am not saying it is impossible, but some real thought and guidance is needed on the more experienced hires."*

And what of the fit of being a future COO, CAO, CoS or business manager? This led me to final question.

Having been a COO, CAO or business manager yourself, or having worked for or alongside one, why do you think ex-military officers often thrive in such roles?

"Loyalty, dedication, willingness to take control of a situation, willingness to make a decision. They understand that even in the best plans, the final 20 per cent is the most challenging, and they retain the focus to see things through with gusto. More so, they have an ability to execute – knowing that you must simply keep putting one foot in front of the other on the path/plan towards completion, but then be willing to pivot when necessary."

"Rigour in forward planning, organisation and execution. The ability to remain flexible and alter plans as needed – not being driven by dogma. We are happy to make decisions on the back of limited information and be accountable for taking them. We are willing to take risks. Finally, our loyalty and trust are ever in question."

"They are strategists who can roll their sleeves up. Soldiers (young and old) help develop an emotional intelligence, which is an important part of building an effective communication style for that company and also for influence above and below."

"A capacity and ability to prioritise. It is, after all, a plate-spinning role, and maintaining enough

focus across a range of tasks is a key skill which most military officers possess. Additionally:

- *Operational judgement. Ability to spot an issue at the earliest opportunity and engage accordingly. We are usually good under pressure and able to maintain a focus on the bigger picture.*
- *Comfort with escalation. It surprised me how reluctant career banking personnel were to highlight shortcomings to senior managers versus those from the armed forces. Military officers are much less afraid of highlighting problems but usually try to mitigate this by developing potential solutions which can be proposed in concise terms in timely fashion.*
- *Generally, we are social creatures and are good at engaging across multiple areas, and are surprisingly well versed, trained and practised in managing diversity."*

Within this feedback, there was a consistent voice focused on delivery, loyalty, managing both upwards and downwards, and so on. All these attributes are well placed in the most demanding COO role. As one person noted, the more senior hires sometimes struggled to migrate successfully into banking. However, I have seen this work, and the success rate seems to be increasing as the demands on the COO's office have grown.

Some suggested that those who had held an adjutant post

would be an almost perfect fit for the COO role. At captain level, an adjutant supports a battalion commander – a lieutenant-colonel managing upwards of a thousand men and women. They would be responsible for manning, discipline, conduct, budget, leadership, training and helping to execute the colonel's vision. This summary of tasks and key responsibilities echoes many COO role specifications I have written. A step up from the adjutant are those who have passed Staff College – a course that helps staff become highly disciplined in the principles of management, project management and planning. These too are a good option if managed carefully and with consideration.

Regardless of the recruitment process and the available talent pool, selection will still come down to one key criterion:

> *"As ever, a well-balanced and honest assessment centred around probably the most important success criterion – fit. Cultural and competency are, in my opinion, the two main areas. If either element is misaligned, then progress will be slow and frustration will follow; if both are in sync, then potential can be reached and careers can flourish."*
>
> FORMER INFANTRY CAPTAIN

"The key to unlocking the door to a successful inter-bank collaborative application is understanding the business motive behind it. Cost saving is a necessary but not sufficient condition. Successful collaborative ventures to date have typically been regulatory driven, such as CLS. A successful business-driven motive would include either some revenue upside for the participants or something that could only be achieved with more than one participant. CGI believes that there are a number of applications in the latter category that could be considered, such as netting of the payments leg of non-FX trades. As a next step, the industry should establish a set of open forums where such initiatives could be tabled."

JERRY NORTON, HEAD OF STRATEGY, FINANCIAL SERVICES, CGI

RESHAPING THE CONVERSATION WITHIN OPERATIONS AND TECHNOLOGY – THE TIME IS NOW

The Q2 2016 Armstrong Wolfe COO forum was attended by over 50 COOs within markets and regional bankwide COOs in London and New York. Participants discussed how the COO community should seek to reshape the conversation with operations and technology.

The debate took place at a time when many banks were realigning their business support functions and, in some cases, taking back direct management of these areas. The discussions were also held in the ever-present shadow of cost and efficiencies, especially in the case of struggling investment banks, where revenues and profits were in sharp decline with no sign of better times to come.

For many years, banks actively invested in low-cost centres and, to a lesser extent, outsourcing, to bring down the capital provision for their infrastructures. Traditionally focused on core operations and technology, this staffing strategy has now extended into risk management and parts of the front office. This was (and is) an understandable strategy, although wage and real estate escalation gathers pace quickly as each location reaches a critical mass of companies. This led many banks to source new locations and territories in the hope of winning a first-entry advantage. Examples of such locations include Poland and other eastern European countries, which offer a mobile, well-educated talent pool within the European Union, as well as being comparatively near Europe's principal financial centres of Europe and London and in a good time zone to bridge the Americas and Asia. In addition, they retain comparatively low compensation and property costs. Centres such as Singapore and Ireland may have been groundbreaking for this headcount migration, but they are no longer viewed as low cost; India remains the leading light on the low-cost spectrum, but is now facing increasing competition from other countries:

> *"Outsourcing has generally been done to save money, not to be more effective or efficient. This has resulted in large distributed teams operating in a waterfall development environment on large code-based applications. Cheap is good, but sometimes it just doesn't work. In my opinion, outsourcing should exist with the more agile onshore smaller development teams. The solution is to take pieces of both, in a balanced portfolio."*

While the effort to outsource to such locations continues, there is a growing opinion that this course of action is not the solution to all cost and efficiency issues. What alternative is there? The answer lies within technology innovation and the point in its own evolution when full automation of any operational process can be achieved. If this innovation is combined with cross-bank collaboration and/or investment in technology and shared utilities of non-proprietary processes, it is possible to move towards the endgame of cost and efficiency. Low-cost centres are used to drive down costs, with the labour and real estate arbitrage, but banks have not realised efficiency gains because antiquated and cumbersome technologies remain in place:

> *"The larger-scale innovation opportunities (particularly around the creation utilities) are found in the areas that banks have already outsourced. This creates difficulties as there are now lots of parties involved and the model looks to erode the rationale for many of the outsourced providers. A turkey rarely votes for Christmas."*

Low-cost centres have delivered good results in the short term, but the technology now exists to deliver advanced processing systems, so banks now need to invest in this to improve efficiency as well as cost. In an environment where capital for such investment is scarce, sharing the cost would appear to be a logical option – and this leads to a creeping sense that we are at a turning point in the evolution of low-cost centre investment and management. Cost demands are pushing us towards cross-bank cooperation – a step that would mark a dramatic shift in the operating model of the industry. As one COO put it:

> *"Technology is the parasite eating the host, where the required medicine is available to cure and rid the body of it, but it is either too costly to access, or once the pill (the solution) is in hand, the host is too fearful to take it."*

This forward-thinking sentiment came up during the debate and had strong supporters. However, there was a pessimistic echo, as some participants were not confident that this collaborative leap could be made. The dissenting voices were not being negative for the sake of it. These COOs were either working or had worked at banks thst held to the belief that there is a competitive advantage to retaining self-built, proprietary technologies. There remains an inherent mistrust between the major players when it comes to the idea of working together on key initiatives, especially those that might deliver an advantage to small or medium-sized institutions (which could see themselves coming together more readily to realise a common goal):

> *"I think organisations are struggling with control and what gets delivered through an innovative construct. Typically, third parties bring capital, concepts and some raw resources, but they generally lack the subject-matter knowledge. Getting this balance right is key."*

The discussion hung on this point for some time. While central to the debate, the issue appears to be not just the use of low-cost centres as part of the staffing, efficiency and cost strategy and what the solution could be. There are also questions about functionalisation (across the bank's various divisions) and the governance and direct ownership of this investment, operational headcount, and ability to mobilise and direct the resource. This would leave many businesses feeling disconnected, with no line of sight into their support functions and no influence over the spend of their investment.

The COO group agreed that it was less a question of cost than one of productivity, the return on investment and the ability to directly influence this significant outlay. "There is a Chinese wall built around the operations and technology empire", one COO explained, "which prevents us from directing its energies to address our business needs effectively." Another COO added: "The invoice for its [operations and technology] services is presented as if a fait accompli, where we are assured we are getting the best possible return on our investment and there exists no viable alternative." This statement had some substance, as this COO had been schooled in operations before moving into the business some 20 years into his banking career. He went on to explain: "This rite of passage seems predicated on the assumption that the only solution is self-build, internal development and in-house operational support, which simply doesn't ring true in today's technologically advanced economic community."

A COO moving from the front office into a lead role in operations contributed to the dialogue: "What makes it more complicated is not the allocation of costs within markets, which are comparatively straightforward, but the allocated costs from elsewhere in group. You intuitively feel these costs, if investigated, would find favour to group and not us, as the end user of their services, which we have little or no influence to change."

Two key questions had taken shape within the debate at this point:

1 Would the interests of the business be better served if it 'owned' and directed operations and technology?

2 Are there better technologies and/or solutions that could offer a different resolution to the traditional in-house, catch-all proposition?

In line with these two themes, there appeared a view that the industry needed to do something to break the status quo, to look beyond the solutions to date and recognise that cross-bank cooperation and collaboration in non-proprietary areas of the infrastructure were no longer theoretical concepts for discussion, but truths that should be exploited.

Where has this idea of finding a mutually beneficial solution come from? Where is there evidence that this breaking of the mould could work? SWIFT and CLS were offered as examples, showing that a spirit of cooperation could be found in previous ventures (although this was more about necessity than a desire for cross-bank innovation and collaboration). This success is not unique within banking, but is sadly one of a small handful of examples banks coming together for the common good. The benefactors of these limited initiatives are clients, investors, the banks themselves and the industry as a whole:

> *"We should be looking to change the processes so that some of the things we are currently doing become obsolete. By going through the automate phase, you can damage the value proposition, as the ultimate saving post-automation isn't large enough to fund unwinding all the automation."*

So why is this the case, when the benefits are understood and widely acknowledged? "The problem is us", explained a global COO Markets of one European bank. "No one else, not the challenge in itself, but us." Another COO added:

> *"The challenge we have, as COOs, is that we*

don't own operations and technology, but we wear the problem. There invariably exists a healthy tension between direct and indirect ownership, although there does exist an overarching focus on cost, efficiencies and discipline. Within the business we have a stated corporate policy that we are committed to adding value to shareholder after allocated costs, which has engendered a greater appreciation of the front-to-back responsibility, although we know still the trader, the heads of desk still hold to a narrow view of what is important, being the customer, price of the trade and its risk profile. The question here is whether we could work with our competitors on areas of potential benefit and whether we need a gun to be held to our head of a regulatory demand or as we find ourselves today, cost, to make it happen. I think we probably do."

Further discussion offered a little more colour to this statement. He went on to explain that banks, certainly the leading institutions, clung to an ill-informed and incorrect assumption that retaining singular control over core operational processes and associated technologies created some form of competitive advantage:

"This misunderstanding was perhaps understandable in days gone by, when cash was plentiful and the direction of travel of the

products was increasingly complex and the technologies were simply not in existence to offer a cross-bank or industry solution. Today however, these technologies do exist, and so does, arguably, the necessity to act."

This is not necessity by law or regulation, but necessity by cost, control and regulation, as well as an increasingly competitive landscape, with 'challenger banks' and the dawn of the Fintech era. It was this statement at the start of the debate that helped frame it perfectly, capturing as it did the spirit of the subject and directing us towards an investigative dialogue. How indeed can the COO community reshape the conversation with operations and technology to deliver a change in direction, if necessity now demands this change? Equally, if this change is needed and was to happen, why does responsibility for driving it lie with the COO community? And do COOs have the power and influence to do so?

The fact is that most COOs are not empowered to initiate such a change, and neither do most directly own the infrastructure. They do, however, carry an influence that flows both up- and downstream. This pivotal position, sitting astride and between the business and its infrastructure, affords the COO community the opportunity to speak for the business at the same time as managing its expectations on success. As a collective … as a community … this voice becomes louder and carries greater influence and authority. If COOs can combine this with objectivity and a desire to do best for the industry, then success could be realised:

"Many organisations have structures whereby a support function's IT costs are allocated to the

support function, which in turn then totals its costs and allocates to businesses and regions."

The group moved towards this position and largely accepted that while this may not happen during the group's tenure, it remained an opportunity – an obligation, even – to try and make happen. "In this case", I asked, "in what areas or common ground, common purpose, non-proprietary, could you sow the seeds for cross-bank, industry-wide collaboration?" Data warehousing and supervision headed the list of such opportunities, with supervision taking top spot, as it was an immediate need. The necessity had been agreed. It was now left to see if this group of executive influencers could find sufficient common purpose to take the first step and perhaps, by drawing this line in the sand, take the industry in a new direction – one that may contribute to its long-term security.

Before finalising this article, I presented it to one of my principal contacts, who added further to the debate:

"Outsourcing was generally done to save money, not to be more efficient or effective. However, while cheap is good, sometimes it just doesn't work. Outsourcing should coexist with the smaller, more agile onshore development teams. The solution is better with pieces of both in a balanced portfolio. Innovation is harder to nurture in a large outsourced waterfall team than it is in a small agile onshore team.

I don't really see an issue of self-build and

proprietary value being friction points.

There is a general feeling that automating these processes is the best solution. However, my view is that we should change the processes so some of the things we are currently doing are obsolete – remove, not automate.

Personally, I would mandate that a cost could only ever be allocated once. Many organisations have structures where support functions IT costs are allocated to the support function which totals its costs and allocates it to businesses and regions. This makes it almost impossible to track which resources are working on what within that function. As support functions are becoming more directly aligned to business units, this should help.

One final point on the new aligned model. I think in many cases now, COOs do own operations – they just haven't realised it yet, and they lack the time and expertise to invest in these groups to help resolve their problems. The COOs are also struggling in some cases as the model shift towards decentralised structure is eroding some of the synergies that had been put in place by the previous global support functions. These are not deal-breakers, but they do need to be acknowledged and resolved."

The realignment of operations and technology

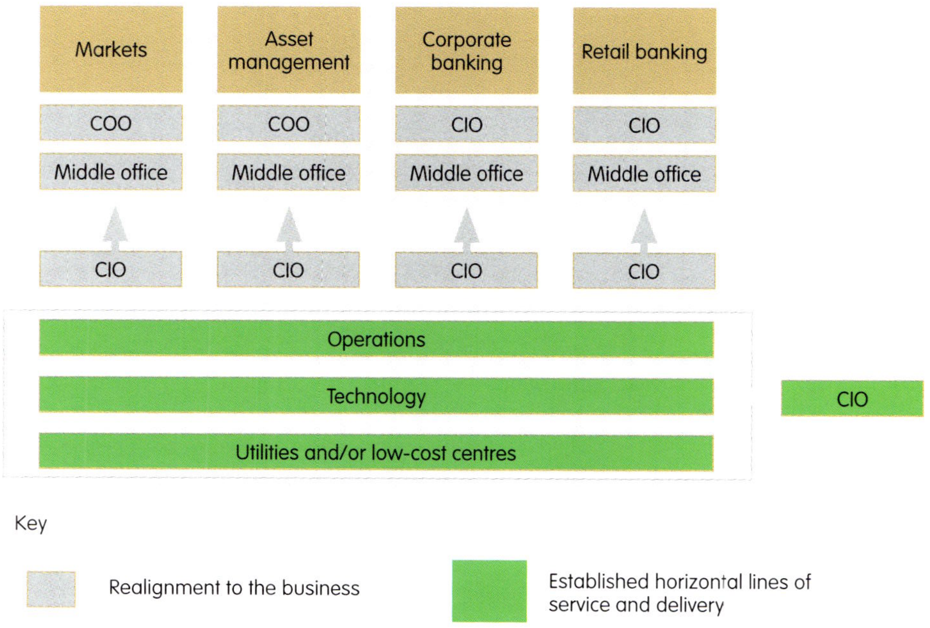

The sphere of influence of the COO

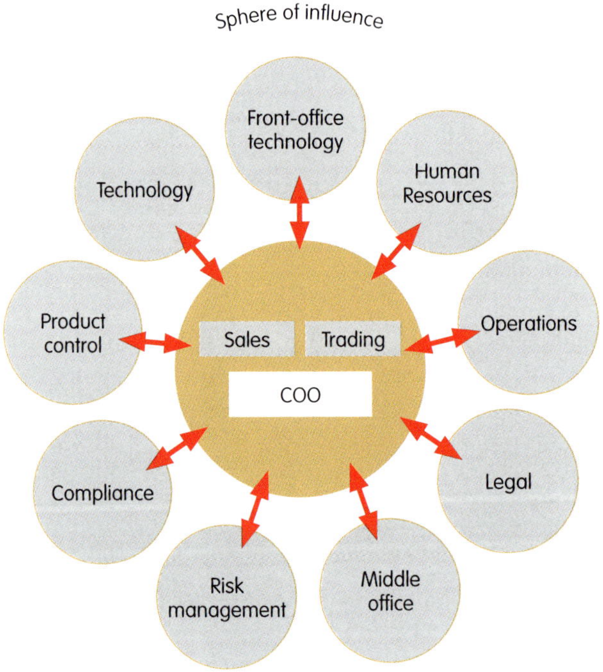

"There is considerable value in careful preparation and planning for the transition ahead."

COACHING THE COO

By Miia Lankinen and Kate Hutchins

The financial crisis has had a profound effect on banks and financial institutions. One consequence of this is that the role of the COO has had to adjust to demonstrate an increasing range of abilities and knowledge to meet the demands of the agenda. The successful COO must have a holistic understanding of the front-to-back business and processes, the complexity of the regulatory environment and risk and compliance issues. In addition, the COO must meet the pressure for increased efficiencies by delivering future operating models and strategy, process management and technology. While it is widely acknowledged within the banking community, and elsewhere in this publication, that the role of the COO carries varying responsibilities from bank to bank and that the weighting of these responsibilities can differ, the issue all COOs face is that they are being asked to achieve more with less.

Understandably, COOs may be concerned how to address these demands, and particularly how to demonstrate their abilities to others in an increasingly competitive market. Through coaching, we help our clients develop the self-awareness they need to identify their achievements and to communicate where they add value, to demonstrate the management competencies they possess that are integral to their success.

Through discussion around career to date, we address themes

such as entrepreneurialism, change management, leadership and strategy. In doing so, we prepare our clients for the challenges ahead, whether that is securing a role in a new organisation, ongoing career development with their current employer or transitioning into a new position.

Our coaching process is unique in that we have an awareness and in-depth appreciation of the challenges and requirements of the industry based on many years of experience supporting the banking sector. As such, we offer individual programmes that recognise not only the personal and professional challenges our clients face, but also the challenges faced by the industry, such as increased governance and regulation.

As proven COOs, clients are leaders with considerable experience in the industry, and they understand how to assess the qualities that contribute to success in others in order to build successful teams and drive the business. They are accomplished career owners who embrace change and take responsibility for managing their career direction; their goals are aligned to the needs of the market. An open-minded approach means they are willing to explore themselves and reflect on their achievements, enabling them to consider a wide range of options for the next challenge.

However, many of them have not often had to consider how to demonstrate and communicate the qualities in themselves that they look for in others. It may have been years since they thought about a change in role or been the interviewee. They recognise that in this different environment there is considerable value in careful preparation and planning for the transition ahead.

Career transitions

Transitioning into a new leadership role can prove a real challenge for even the most seasoned executive. With increased expectations and pressure to make an impact, while delivering quick wins and building new relationships, the first few months in a new role are critical to success and sustainable performance.

According to the Corporate Executive Board, almost half of executives struggle or underperform in new roles. McKinsey has similar research, indicating that only 40 per cent of newly hired or promoted senior executives are considered successful after their first 18 months. This is partly due to organisations failing to manage transitions effectively; and partly to individuals not being aware of their transition risks. As well as a new role and job scope, transitions often involve a fresh corporate culture and business model, new stakeholders, peers and networks; a different geographic location and culture; and a number of family adjustments. This is where working with a coach on identifying risks and planning for the transition – ideally before the new role begins – can make all the difference.

Returning to work after an extended career break is a special case of transition that can feel particularly overwhelming. Here, coaching can focus on exploring the decision to return to work and preparing for the road ahead.

Whether it is to gain the confidence to return to a career, to quickly understand the organisational culture and required mindset and behavioural changes, or to gain clarity on the strategic priorities and where and how to make the biggest difference in the new role, transition coaching supports and accelerates the transition process. It provides a positive focus at a time of instability while empowering individuals to own their career direction.

Through a successful programme of career coaching, we effectively build a bridge that allows clients to move from where they are now to where they want to be. This is particularly relevant to today's COOs, who face myriad challenges when demonstrating to other members of the C-suite the value they bring. COOs recognise that they need to work at self-promotion and communication to increase understanding of their role and the benefit it brings to the organisation. Through discussion and exploration, client are able to review and evaluate their position, considering a number of factors – both personal and socio-economic – which enable them to cross the bridge. Career management gives the COO the support and preparation to ensure they communicate who they are effectively and gives them the opportunity to make meaningful choices about their future.

Miia Lankinen – ASIA Practice Head of Career Management

"In the current environment, new business dynamics are redefining old roles and creating new ones. Senior and executive-level roles today are increasingly complex, requiring a wider set of competence than before. This presents an opportunity for our clients to revisit their career goals and to consider how to best position themselves for the next move. We are here to help them do just that."

Armstrong Wolfe offers a comprehensive career management service designed to align skills and career aspirations with the demand across the market. We explore the career process with our clients and ensure they make effective and constructive decisions. We aim to maximise the opportunity for success by helping individuals understand their competencies, how to translate and communicate them, and how to present them through a CV and at an interview.

Our approach is structured and held on a one-to-one basis, considering individual needs. A tailored programme that takes into account ambitions and a pragmatic assessment of market opportunities is designed for each client. We provide support for those seeking to move from one permanent role to another, during the transition after a successful application to a new role, and advice for those seeking to get back into the workplace, be it on an interim or permanent basis.

This service can be provided as a complete package or in component parts based on the client's need. The core service consists of the following:

- An initial conversation to explore the client's career goals and interests and assess the support required.
- Thorough review of client's CV, communicating her or his behavioural strengths and commercial value.
- LinkedIn profile optimisation review.
- 1:1 coaching to prepare for the interview process and follow-up support for the application process.
- Interview questions, practise and feedback.
- Recommendations.

Kate Hutchins - UK Practice Head of Career Management

Additional services available:

- Occupational personality questionnaire to ensure the best alignment of competencies with business requirements, followed by a feedback and coaching session.
- 1:1 transition coaching for those returning to workplace after a break, or following a successful application.

"The financial services sector continues to face challenges that have dramatically affected the employment landscape. Our service ensures that clients are able to communicate that they can demonstrate the competencies, behaviour and values required to promote integrity and trust in the industry. Our approach is unique in that it harnesses a depth of specialist industry knowledge together with a wealth of experience in supporting individuals through times of change."

TELEPHONE

"A view through the lens of commerciality and objectivity is a key attribute that the front-office business manager could bring to the role of head of operations."

SKILL SET MIGRATION FOR THE COO

Target operating models within global operations

The need for commercial leadership and functional objectivity – step in the COO.

With evolution and with the demands of cost and control forced rapidly into an uncomfortable marriage, the profile of the operations head has had to change in response to these dynamics. Commerciality and an ability to look through a different lens to deliver entrepreneurial solutions are recognised requirements of such an executive post. Outsourcing and/or relocation partnering to in-house or external piecemeal technology solutions and improvements will no longer meet the demand for either wholesale change or the savings required for individual banks and the industry as a whole to achieve sustainability. The current model and its trajectory will simply not deliver the required cost reductions over the long term.

Into this space steps the front-office business manager – the COO. An increasing number of banks have appointed a head of operations from within the business, but such appointments have raised eyebrows. Surely this person cannot understand the intricacies of the operational processes and lacks the management experience necessary for overseeing a global function?

This may be true, but what they do understand – the accomplished ones – is a need to look beyond the present, limited, operational horizon and question the viability of the current business plan. They will then seek to design and execute a new vision – one not tied to any legacy strategy and with no emotional attachment to the historic need for the business to build, invest in, buy in and own its front-to-back operational processes.

A view through the lens of commerciality and objectivity is a key attribute that the front-office business manager could bring to the role of head of operations or principal middle-office head. Equally important are the decision-making criteria of the appointee, as he or she will have to understand and embrace the imperative of such an appointment, moving swiftly past the emotional matter of shifting from an executive role in the front office to one in the back. Once focused on the mission of the role, which will lead to a better business model and sustainable profitability, the decision should be an easy one. By prioritising pragmatism over ideology, it should become apparent to the more enlightened that this is an opportunity for making a real difference. Mid- to long-term career opportunities will not be in short supply for those who deliver in such a role.

Target operating models within global operations and opportunities in leadership for the front-office business manager

Leading change from front to back

While many COOs venture down their career paths with a sense of shrinking opportunity, some have taken advantage of this evolutionary moment to move from front-office roles into those of principal leadership within operations. The accountability of control front to back and the demands to reduce costs are now the leading items on most agendas. Thus, as businesses seek to align themselves ever closer to the infrastructure, transferring experience and patronage from within the business into a role supporting it has become increasingly commonplace. So, what enables this talent to be successful in such a different role?

Background organisational analysis

The following organisational charts give examples of the operational process and leadership alignment in principal financial market franchises. The interpretation of these alignments has been gathered from those currently or previously in operations leadership positions; while they are not wholly accurate, therefore, they are representative. They show that while no two banks have exactly the same structure and organisation, there are themes that run through the market:

- The continual move towards the use of utilities and investment in near-shore capabilities to support more sensitive products and/or to mitigate the effects of compensation increases (and therefore loss in savings) at maturing low-cost centres, such as in India, due to increased competition for experienced talent.
- The integration of cross-sector operations processes, such as financial markets, wealth, private banking and asset management (although, having spent millions on this horizontal functionalisation, some banks are now dismantling it).
- The evolution of the middle-office manager as the 'new executive' of operations and/or the movement of middle office into front office, reporting to the front-office COO.
- The establishment of clearing and collateral business support groups (independent from fixed income and/or equity operations).

- The role of the operations COO (or other) as the/a global control officer responsible for governance, control and transformation (within operations and/or technology).

Research shows that head of (markets/IB) operations is a stand-alone mandate reporting to a head of operations and technology and/or to the COO when in a divisional construct at markets/IB level. However, when in an integrated, cross-divisional alignment, the head of operations may report into a divisional CIO or into a group head of operations and/or group COO. There appears to be no consistent target operating model, and in many cases the model itself has changed multiple times within a bank, as leadership struggles to meet the varied demands of cost, efficiency and regulation.

Additional observations

While the Investment Banking Operations executive and leadership teams are charged with delivering common services to the sales and trading business, how they are aligned varies significantly between the leading financial market and/or capital market franchises. The exact alignment may vary for several reasons, including:

- Regional bias of the business.
- Business weighting across fixed income and equities.
- Maturity of the infrastructure.
- Key personalities and organisational preferences.
- Corporate commitment to off/near shoring (captive or vendor).

Armstrong Wolfe's research into the present alignment of operations outlines a relatively uniform progression across the market in the evolution of the target operating model:

Phase 1: Fixed income and equities operational product heads (including front to back from middle office, through confirmation into settlement); global heads of shared services/control, change management and cross-product regional heads of operations.

Phase 2: Global heads of derivatives and securities operations; global heads of shared services, change management and cross-product regional heads of operations and appointment of a global control officer (as COO or other).

Phase 3: As above, with the migration of core operations headcount to low-cost centres (off- or onshore) and, more recently, outsourcing.

Phase 4: (Present state) evolution of the middle-office function as global product heads (be they a 'fixed income – equities' or 'derivatives – securities' model), with mature hub locations for core processes, single domain/product change functions, with a separation of clearing and collateral management.

Phase 5: Where now? Reduced revenues and the impact of regulation have led to an increasingly common and shared view that a seismic shift is needed within the industry if a sustainable model and acceptable cost ratio (for operations and technology) is to be achieved. Challenging the status quo, looking beyond banking for

Key for the evolution of the operations chart on the following two pages

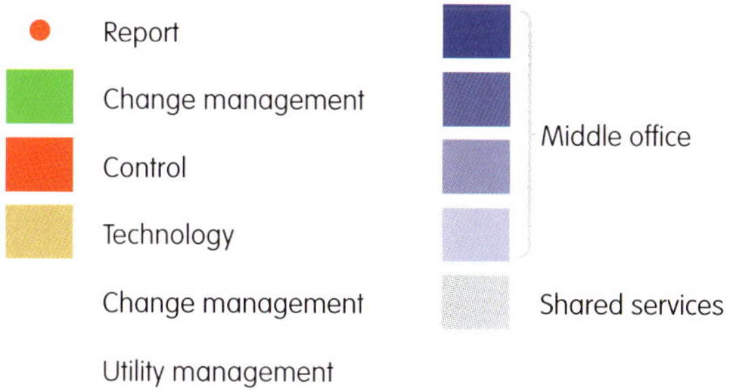

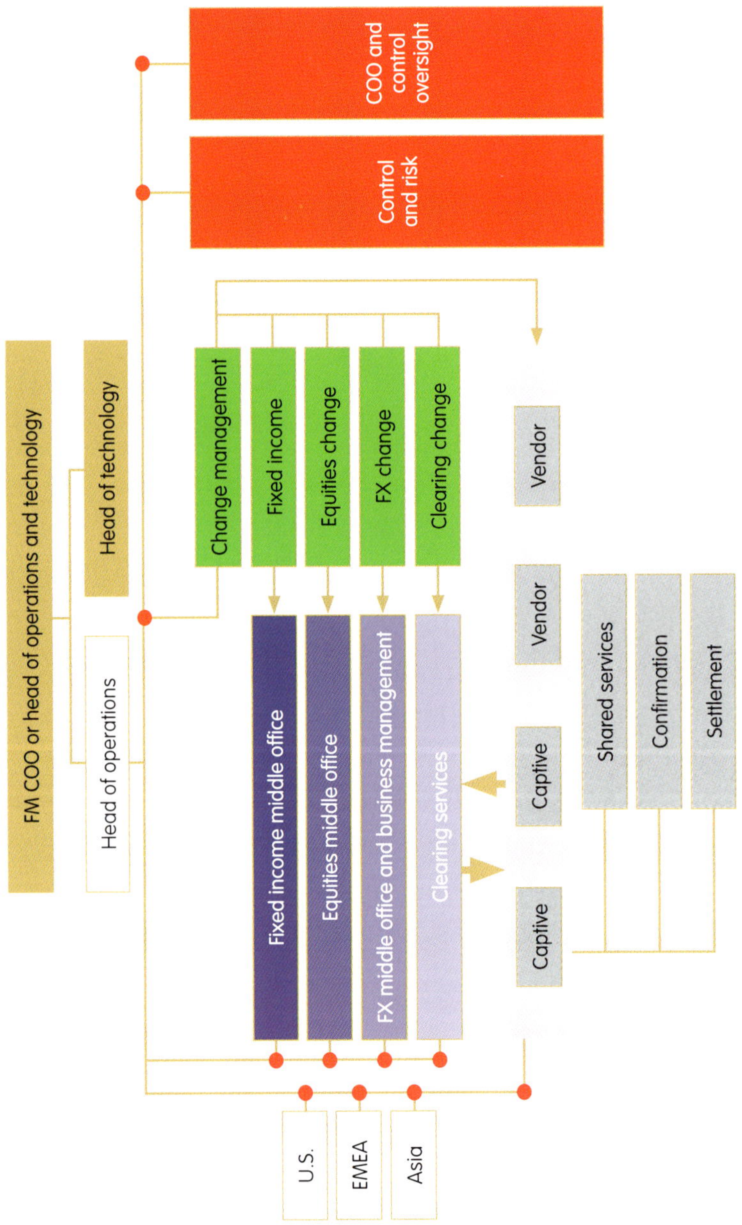

Evolution of the IB operations target operating model: model 1

Evolution model on of the IB operations target operating model: model 2

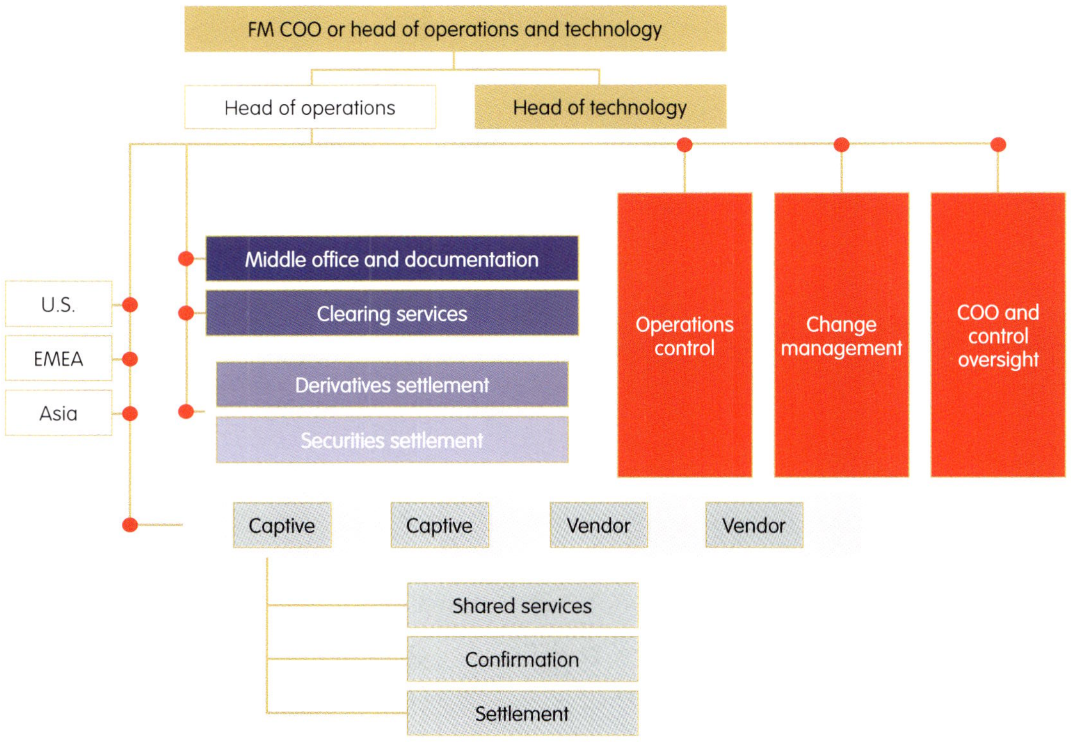

solutions and new technologies, and cross-industry collaboration will all be needed to meet this shared objective. How to mobilise an industry, specifically this industry, to produce a common and shared solution is perhaps the greatest challenge of all.

Moving parts: the middle office is moving forward

Aligned to the changing emphasis of the middle-office role, the middle office – or component parts of it – have been moved to front office, to report to the front-office COO. This is driven in no small part by control and the need to bring this key area of process (and people) risk closer to the front end.

Most banks have reviewed, evaluated and in some cases executed this organisational change, moving this operational process into front office. Present market challenges around cost management, regulation, control and clearing are impacting the present and future alignment and the target operating models of investment banking operations functions. Banks have addressed these challenges in different ways, some of which are outlined below.

Cost management vs risk and control

To varying degrees, banks have embraced the low-cost centre model, where the benefit of migrating headcount to low-cost centres is unquestionable. Whether this is on- or offshoring, or vendor or captive utilities, a variant of this operational strategy is now in place in all banks. Strategies on such initiatives vary significantly, from corporate and group strategies and rigid adherence, through to alignments at divisional level and, in some cases, those influenced by executive preferences and personalities.

Central to the decision-making process are the savings to be realised, weighed against the level of acceptable risk within this headcount migration. More recently control – and implications of failures in control – have played a role in defining this strategy within the first line, just as the implications of regulatory change are doing so downstream and into operations, such as Dodd-Frank and clearing demands, and defined requirements on the front-to-back business proposition and processes. This has provided support for some of the more complex operational processes to be brought back onshore. It has also provided confirmation for those that have not yet moved that they will remain where they are.

Cost savings vs risk mitigation

How these demands are to be accommodated with the low-cost and/or outsourcing strategies in most banks is not yet clear, as internal debate continues on these extenuating factors. Entering 2016, the markets were cornered by compressed revenues, plateauing costs and enhanced regulation. The default position within operations and technology was to realise cost savings relatively quickly through offshoring and/or outsourcing. However, this endgame strategy is now being questioned, and it is generally recognised that a longer-term and more commercial solution is needed.

In this context, those holding fast to quantified savings find themselves in debate with the subjective and qualitative view as to the overall benefit. Why? Firstly, the level of enhanced operational risk and loss of control incurred from the aggressive pursuit of a low-cost centre strategy is often cited as a counterbalance to pure price and cost effectiveness. Secondly, it reduces the cost to a certain level, and is better than the present situation, but is not the end solution.

In some cases, banks have responded to the risk and control issue by establishing onshore locations to service some of the more complex processes, although at a higher cost than if they were based in India or Manila, for example. The argument for this is that the increased comparative cost is justified when taking into consideration the enhanced risk involved in supporting certain businesses and products. In this case the issue over legacy and the ongoing cost remains.

Not surprisingly, with so many banks struggling to maintain margin and profit, the pressure on cost is pushing the debate to the forefront of discussion between the business and operations:

> *"Exactly what part of my operational service do you want me to stop or exactly what level of enhanced operational risk are you willing to accept if I have to (a) move headcount (b) remove head count?"*

This statement (or a variant of it) is one that many operations executives would have used during discussions about ways of driving down costs, concerned as they are about the enhanced levels of risk involved in this period of sustained change and aggressive cost management and reduction. This is even more relevant as accountability for control failures is often more readily (and rightly) allocated to departmental managers.

Control and cost: an unhappy marriage

The debate is not about empire building or parochial desires to hold on to headcount, but is rather about exactly what is right for the business during this phase of market change. What we have gathered from market interaction is that while core operational processes – be they simple or mature – are well placed to be moved into low-cost centres, not all processes that are theoretically capable of being moved into low-cost centres should be subject to that move.

The focus of the debate tends to be 'where or what next?', with banks looking into previously untouched areas/processes to find savings, moving processes from principal business centres into utilities. This is especially apparent in middle office and an assessment of risk and front-office components. However, it is still somewhat short of the leap required to revolutionise the way the banking industry supports its sales and trading activity.

Time for fundamental change: the art of the possible?

The industry must change because the present operating model is not sustainable. This statement captures the essence of conversations being held industry-wide. It has long been recognised that the present cost burden of a bloated, overpaid infrastructure (headcount mainly within operations and technology) is unsustainable. Strong revenues had once been able to carry it, but this is no longer the case, and banks are being forced to look internally and aggressively at their operating models. The more enlightened are also looking externally and to the art of the possible. There are many examples of cross-bank and cross-industry cooperation, demonstrating collaboration in establishing centralised operational services. SWIFT is testament to this, as was the market need for CLS. This does, however, still tinker with the main issue, where "creation of a bank-wide, industry-wide, industry-owned settlement utility would be nirvana", as one COO has suggested.

Is this possible? Of course it is – the technology exists. The issue is whether the courage and willingness at individual banks also exist. It appears that the simple economic imperative to make such a leap may force the hands of the sceptics.

BANCO DO

BRASIL S.A.

"Can you be 'too experienced' for a role if you are willing to apply yourself in a dedicated manner to the opportunity?"

AGEISM IN GLOBAL BANKING

Too experienced or too old?

Below the corporate face of banking rests a growing pool of highly experienced but unemployed bankers. They are the casualties of the turmoil in the financial services sector over the last seven years. Their unemployment is the by-product of the much-advertised effort of the banking sector to drive down costs, with redundancy programmes removing excess managerial headcount and distributing this floating resource to the open market.

Coupled with this (for those still in employment) are sustained pressures, falling reward, public animosity towards the sector and the sense that the high days of banking have been and gone. Not surprisingly, an increasing number of the experienced managers of the sector are taking stock of their career. Upon this reflection some are now seeking alternative options, outside banking. As one previous global CAO markets, with 30 years' experience although still only in his early fifties, states:

> *"I see a lot of experienced individuals taking the opportunity to pursue alternative careers and make lifestyle choices. They have become*

disillusioned with the financial sector, so are using their experience (and redundancy money) to do other things. This in my opinion is creating a brain drain from the sector. Whilst those seeking re-employment into banking may well be considered casualties, the banks have also given many an unforeseen opportunity and choice, and many of them are turning their backs on the City. Many think good, experienced individuals will become scarcer. I have seen many friends struggle with re-entering the market, being told they are 'too experienced' with this or that role, whereas others have found interim employment within a contract role, invariably engaged to undertake tasks aligned to regulatory change."

This shift must be put in context. While the overall population in the banking sector has shrunk, many of the more junior staff post-redundancy have managed to be absorbed back into it. It is mainly those at a more senior level, with more than 25 years' experience in banking and previously holding appointments at director to managing director level, who are finding re-entry into the permanent employment market challenging. It is widely acknowledged that the banking sector was overpopulated at the executive level and in need of pruning, so this cannot be a surprise for many.

Such cost-cutting programmes successfully met the expectations of shareholders demanding action by the banks to drive down cost and reward. However, unforeseen at this time was the mid- to long-term impact of regulatory change and additional demands from shareholders that banks establish a stronger risk and control framework to avoid the calamities of the recent past. The challenge for all banks is to meet the demands of this ever-changing environment with a reduced headcount, a significant loss of intellectual capital and a lack of seasoned leadership.

Traditionally the banking sector had filled such transformation and project demands for intermediate help with additional internal resources and floating headcount or by engaging management consultancies. Now banking has few internal resources to draw upon to manage change programmes, and the cost of engaging consultancies on a long-term basis works counter to the objective of effectively managing the bottom line.

However, we need to be aware of the view of those who have been let go and have found themselves in the unenviable position of being unemployed at a comparatively late point in their career. Some argue that these seasoned individuals have been paid handsomely for many years and their present hardship should thus be weighed in comparison to those perceived less fortunate outside banking. But the majority of these individuals were not leaders; they were senior employees who had been servants to the business, dedicating themselves to careers in non-direct revenue-generating roles such as COO, business management, risk, finance, technology and operations. They are part of the sector that has suffered a dramatic decline in fortunes, but certainly they were not culpable. Many high-profile bankers who led respectable businesses have become casualties of market change, but they are often in a position to retire without having to seek further employment. The middle to senior management of the non-direct revenue-generating world, on the other hand, may have been paid comparatively well, but they find themselves in middle age with family and personal commitments based on consistency of income. They are not able to take early retirement.

A high percentage of this talent pool recognises that the banking sector is now in a different phase of reward and opportunity. Most would happily take secure employment at a significantly reduced financial reward and accept that this compensation profile is unlikely to return to what it was pre-credit crunch. Surprisingly, many have found this willingness – combined with their experience – to be a detrimental factor. This is often an uncomfortable experience: this talent pool was often previously the hiring manager – the client of recruitment and search agencies. Now they find themselves the candidates, seeking guidance and help. They find their hopes of prospective employment dashed by questionable feedback such as being considered 'too senior for the role', 'too experienced', 'possibly institutionalised'. In some cases their common sense with regards to compensation is met with cynicism that their own pricing is short-term pragmatism, which will unfold as unrealistic mid- to long-term expectations.

Can you be 'too experienced' for a role if you are willing to apply yourself in a dedicated manner to the opportunity? Is hiring someone at a lower financial reward than that person previously received beneficial to the individual in securing gainful employment and to the employer in securing talent cost effectively? Many of these arguments lack substance and could be defined as weak excuses. It is at the very least debatable that the banking sector is suffering from discrimination and ageism in relation to this seasoned group of professionals.

Unlike the 2005 legislation that sought to reduce and mitigate ageism for those in their early to mid years of employment, it appears we also need protection for those at the mid to latter period of their careers. Many would consider the banking sector, as it navigates troubled times, to be in great need of the experience of those who have battle scars from many years in the industry. Surely transformation and change agendas can be more ably handled by such experience, and regulators, the public and politicians would feel more comfortable in dealing with 'silver-haired' executives.

The challenge for those out of work is that there will not be any overnight change in market sentiment or perception. Indeed, it may not even happen in the next few years. Unlike in Asia, where age and gravitas are perceived as primary attributes for senior executive roles, western capitalist culture has a career orientation that suggests banking is a young man's game, especially within financial markets.

Need this be the case? Is this the case?

As we ran towards the end of the last century, there was a sea change in banking that demanded a new breed of professionally qualified people. This was aligned to extraordinary growth in the sector. Many were fast-tracked to directorship at a young age. This built an expectation of such advancement in those further down the corporate ladder. As a consequence, there now exists an ageing directorate and a talent block below them – and both are positioned in a shrinking sector for opportunities. In addition, people are living longer, working longer and able to add value longer. Despite this, only a very small percentage of those now employed in the banking sector are over 50 years old.

It is the alignment of these factors that the industry needs to address in dealing with this growing problem. It needs to work out how it can retain, use and reuse this ageing population, while maintaining opportunity based on merit for the rising talent and the leaders of tomorrow. Career fast-tracking and/or the migration and variety within jobs, slowing down advancement, may serve this purpose as long as expectations are carefully managed. However, while this will in part solve the problem, it may give rise to other issues within a sector where diversity and opportunity are key to attracting upper-quartile talent. This could also be aligned to changing working practises – it is not a lack of opportunity for gainful employment that is causing experienced people to be out of work, but the nature of that employment. Change management is needed to bridge the gap between the requirement to reduce cost and to meet the obligations of the regulators and control. It is into this gap that the resting pool of talent could be appropriately and ably employed.

For many, this will be an emotional challenge and will require a mindset shift from the former security of permanent employment, rank and title and the structure of the corporate ladder. This is because banks may hire individuals on a contract or interim basis to deliver against defined tasks and objectives. In doing so, they keep these people off the permanent headcount while securing relevant and proven experience to manage a programme of work, in many cases at a margin of the cost of engaging a traditional management consultancy. To do this, these individuals will have to repackage themselves, commoditise their experience and keep themselves up to date with the moving parts in a dynamic market place. Being enthusiastic, energised but still humble at interview will be key to securing such opportunities.

Some, like Rob Cook (46), who runs the Interim division of Armstrong Wolfe, recently made this career shift, resigning as EMEA COO for Emerging Markets at JPMorgan to become a professional interim. He is now working within Armstrong Wolfe Interim as a consultant on various assignments in London:

"I reviewed my career and realised my strengths, and where I enjoyed myself had always been

working within transformation. Additionally, dedicating my life and career to climbing the corporate ladder simply did not excite me. I wanted to create a lifestyle which had balance and reward and met my desires for working within a change management capacity. With financial services companies being more open to and in need of flexible resources, stepping out of permanent employment was not so much a risk as a calculated decision to make myself available for employment opportunities that would meet my needs and match my skills."

Rob saw the possibility of mobilising this dormant, underused senior management and executive talent:

"By harvesting this talent that has found itself out of work not by choice, repackaging them and offering new employment options, whilst at the same time offering flexibility for them to work on assignments for stated periods in the year, as they sought. Conversely, it is a cost-effective solution to meet many banks' needs to engage experienced, subject-matter experts, whilst not adding to permanent headcount or engaging expensive consultancies – the latter more likely than not possessing less direct, in-business experience."

Discrimination may exist, but opportunities are available for both the client and candidate to realise mutual benefit for those with many years in banking and finding themselves out of work. How both parties might position themselves to realise this benefit within an evolving and changing market and a growing and ageing population is unfolding. Marrying the two – client demand and subject-matter supply – is precisely where an opportunity exists. Through seeking to match experience with business need, an employer may be accused of positive discrimination in favour of those senior bankers actively seeking work. Conversely, they may simply be recognised for providing a much-needed service that releases the dormant experience and provides it to the banks on merit alone, not age or other factor.

Within this talent pool, there are a growing number of former COOs and business managers. Much of the work is related to the direct impact on the business. It demands someone with experience working within that business, alongside sales and trading, as well as someone who truly understands the journey from pre-trade, through trade to settlement. In these circumstances, the skills and experience of a COO or business manager are well suited. It may not be a career option, but it does offer a route back into employment for those carrying years of valued experience. Despite this, it does not address the creeping phenomena that age is a disadvantage to career advancement, especially for those whose determination to keep working is being thwarted by perception rather than reality. The silver-haired COO may not be extinct, but it is a rare beast indeed!

"To accommodate this challenge in the mid to long term, some are diversifying and hiring at more junior levels, attracting prospective candidates into treasury who would formerly have been only attracted into a risk or trading environment."

A LEAP OF FAITH

Market volatility and regulatory demands drive COOs to think laterally for talent

One of the key challenges for any business is meeting the staffing demands for precise technical skill-sets at peak times: if one bank is looking, they are probably all looking. In new areas such as 1LOD, being first into this area may well deliver first-starter disadvantage, allowing the development of a subject-matter talent pool for the followers to access. In response to this, COOs have begun to think laterally about how to meet these demands, asking themselves: "If the person for this role does not exist, what skills and experiences would be useful or necessary in role? Where can I find the right person with the right experience that we could leverage and train into this new role, or complement a team in which talent is in short supply?" The following is an example within liquidity risk.

In these turbulent times, risk management is a key concern for both board members and shareholders. Recent events in the global banking system have demonstrated the importance of identifying threats that could have a devastating impact on a business. The need to balance risk and control to enhance value to stakeholders and prevent loss has never been more apparent. While many areas of banking are facing headcount reduction, risk management and change within risk's infrastructure are not under pressure to reduce headcount. Indeed, the contrary position is found, with high demands on risk management leading to a market-wide search for experienced talent. Why? Enhanced levels of risk and new demands placed upon it through regulation may combine with lack of experience in areas of new regulation, and this may require the strengthening of the Chief Risk Officer's function. Hiring capable talent is central to meeting this demand.

At a time of such uncertainty, many risk managers are considering the personal risks of moving and are unsurprisingly seeking a premium to make a change in response to this career risk assessment and that the supply-and-demand equation is presently in their favour. These factors have ushered in compensation increases that are countercyclical to rest of the staffing market. The value of any offer is balanced against the role itself, pay and, importantly, market position and robustness of the bank making the offer. The banks that have managed their way through turbulent times in comparative good order are therefore well placed to both retain and secure talent within the risk management space.

The hunt for treasury talent

The demand is not just within the traditional risk areas of credit, market and operational risk management. Those experienced in liquidity risk are arguably in higher demand than all others, as banks struggle with market volatility and funding constraints. This is tied to the talent gap created by the flow of regulations and the need to understand, address and implement the necessary policies and procedures arising from them.

Transferability of the risk mind and skill-set from one risk discipline to another has put further pressures on the risk sector. While regulatory pressure on managing liquidity risks is valid, the more pressing practical problem is how to meet liquid capital needs while ensuring profitability in a time of low margins. Strategies for fine-tuning liquidity risk management practices appear to be a) liquidity risk policy development and b) liquidity management – arguably the key to better business agility and profitability. Here, experience and reliability are essential, and securing and retaining the right staff are placing acute demands on treasury functions as they seek to upskill their departments.

Always the hub, now the nucleus

Treasury had always been seen as the hub of the organisation, but post-credit crunch, its role has become enhanced, more complex and significantly more important from both an internal and external perspective. Specifically, the impact of regulations relating to capital allocation, fund requirement and the internal demands of business heads is changing the profile of individuals required by treasury. Some talent may develop from within it, but the new skill-sets required demand that the treasury function must import aligned skills from global markets and/or aligned trading and risk management areas. Funding, balance sheet management, capital management and allocation, and liquidity risk management all demand an upskilling to allow the treasury function to successfully meet the requirements of the business and match the requirements of the regulators.

Perhaps the greatest area of demand is within liquidity risk management, which many business heads see as the new market risk. Previously there was a requirement for reporting on historical events, which could be delivered through either the finance function or managed by those of finance heritage and training. However, the need for stress-testing liquidity ratios and to meet the demands of, for example, the head of equity for a more complex understanding of the implications on their business funding and capital requirements, means that people from a much stronger quantitative and risk background are required. This leaves most banks searching for talent from a limited and underqualified pool. Many banks have little choice but to identify aligned skills from other areas to strengthen their treasury function.

Route to talent and its implications

With treasury becoming a far more business-aligned function, and the evolution of liquidity risk management, banks will be forced to look into global markets and aligned trading areas to source talent with relevant experience. The immediate impact of this is to bridge the compensation gap between those paid a premium within global markets and the traditional treasury pay scales. Some banks are already halfway through this process, which has led to huge disparities within treasury compensation structures, particularly at the more senior levels.

It is estimated by some banks that even if the headcount remains flat, the allocated budget for treasury department compensation will increase by around 20%. This is partly due to migration of internal talent from global markets on parity – many banks are already concerned about losing treasury talent to an increasingly competitive market. This is accompanied by the need for many banks to seek external talent, where demand exceeds supply and manifests itself in compensation escalation. The price per hire has risen and continued to do so through the post-bonus period.

To accommodate this challenge in the mid to long term, some are diversifying and hiring at more junior levels, attracting prospective candidates into treasury who would formerly have been only attracted into a risk or trading environment. However, this remains a longer-term solution to an immediate need, and compensation for those with experience will escalate.

The three key skills in demand are as follows:

1 Those who are able to demonstrate an in-depth technical understanding of the business and its products to respond to increasing demands from the product and business heads.
2 Those with an in-depth and technical understanding of regulatory matters and those able to respond to evolving and changing circumstance.
3 Quantitative skills and in-depth understanding of key risk indicators.

Compensation

Our research shows that the EMEA regional treasury head is closely aligned to the reward of the functional and global heads of funding and liquidity/capital management, although research at VP to MD levels demonstrates a significant variance between 2013/2014 and 2015/2016 compensation levels and bonus payments.

This period of flux has often led to an incumbent at D to MD level hiring much-needed staff/managers and having to offer more than their own package to secure them. This is only palatable in the very short term and sets a justifiable expectation for a commensurate adjustment at year end. Furthermore, compensation can vary significantly depending upon where treasury roles reside – within the business, risk or finance.

Conclusion

This challenge is not in isolation. It can be found market-wide and represents a potentially significant staffing issue for many functions today, such as when the treasury function comes under pressure to upskill accordingly. Alongside the current demand to manage cost, there is an acknowledgement of the need for an increase in treasury budgets to enable it to attract and retain its talent.

In the short term, the skill gap can/must be filled through the migration of talent from other areas (such as market risk) internally and externally. One treasury COO commented that it felt as if you were 'robbing Peter to pay Paul'. However, in line with the further evolution of treasury and the demands upon it, mid- to long-term staffing requirements can only be fulfilled by a disciplined approach to attracting and securing emerging talent into a function with an enhanced role, level of importance and complexity.

APPENDIX

Armstrong Wolfe chief operating officer (COO) forums: 2015-2016

COO Forum: 'Cooperation and Collaboration: Seeking Common Solutions to Cost and Complexity'

November 14, 2016 - New York
Held at Ernst & Young LLP

COO Forum: 'A Problem Shared is a Problem Halved: Cross-bank Cooperation within Non-proprietary Infrastructures'

July 13, 2016 - New York
July 20, 2016 - London
Both held at Ernst & Young LLP

COO Forum: 'The Art of the Possible: Target Operating Models within Banking'

April 20, 2016 - New York
Held at Societe Generale

April 13, 2016 - London
Held at Commerzbank

COO Forum: 'Fostering the Future Leadership of the Markets' COO Community'

December 3, 2015 - New York
Held at Barclays
November 25, 2015 - London
Held at JP Morgan

COO Forum: 'Industry Utilities Designed, Owned and Run by the Industry'

September 22, 2015 - London
Held at Societe Generale

COO Forum: 'The Evolution of the Financial Markets' COO'

June 1, 2015 - London
Held at Credit Suisse

COO Forum: 'Defining the Indefinable: The Evolution of the Front-office Control Officer'

March 1, 2015 - London
Hosted by Armstrong Wolfe

GLOSSARY

Organisation and governance

Limited companies

The simplest form of commercial organisation is a *sole trader*. This person and her or his business activities are one and the same – they owning the business, controlling the business and making all decisions regarding the strategy of the business. Next we have *partnerships* – this is where the business is owned and managed by several partners, and like sole traders, there is little to distinguish between where their business ends and they start. Then *companies/corporations* were invented. Under this structure, the business itself has a legal identity, separate from that of its owners. That's where the name corporation comes from – 'corps' is the French for body – it has its own legal life. Someone who is the owner of a business and who is set up as a sole trader or partner can have all of his or her possessions taken to pay for the debts of the business – that's the piece where it's hard to see where the business/personal life is separated. Owner of a limited company, however, have their possessions protected, as only the money they have given to the company in return for their 'share' of it can be taken to pay debts. If the owner spends £200,000 to set up the company, that's all they can lose. If the company racks up debts of £1 million and the debtors want their money back, they go to the company – a separate legal entity – not the owner. Shares are certificates evidencing the fact that someone owns part/all of a company. Shares are also known as stocks or equities. The money companies use to operate is called *capital*; the money given to a company in return for a share in it is called *share capital*. The owners are called *shareholders*.

CEO and executive board

In a small business, such as a sole trader, all the decisions and activities are performed by the sole trader only. In a bigger business, the owners (shareholders) ensure that their company is well run by splitting up the tasks. The business is run by the CEO and his/her management team. They handle the formation and implementation of strategy. The CEO and all the management team are employees of the company – known as the executive board.

Directors and board of directors

The shareholders appoint directors to check that the important aspects of running a company are being performed satisfactorily by the CEO and his or her team and to set the strategic direction for the company. The directors can be employed by the company, in which case they are known as *executive directors*, or can be external to the company, in which case they are non-executive. These non-executive directors are chosen because they have skills and experiences that the company can use. So for example if you and I were setting up a company to make and sell 'widgets' we may decide to have as directors the world's leading 'widget' expert from a renowned university and an expert from a law firm. The directors organise themselves into a board of directors, and a team captain is appointed by the shareholders, called the *chairman*.

Auditors

The shareholders appoint an independent external *auditor* to review the books and records being produced by the company and to ensure their accuracy – to detect if the staff are 'cooking the books': stealing from the company and generating fictitious accounting records.

Banks

Retail bank

A retail bank's customers are the public. The bank keeps the customer's cash safe and secure and provides means to get it back (e.g., ATMs). The bank also provides facilities to pay bills (chequebook, debit card, direct debit, etc.) and makes loans (e.g., credit cards, mortgages).

Commercial bank

A commercial bank's customers are businesses. The bank keeps assets such as cash and securities and provides means to retrieve the assets and pass them on to others.

Investment bank

An investment bank's customers are companies. They fall into two categories:

- *Those that need money*. Companies need money to either start or grow their businesses (the money companies use in this way is called *capital*).

- *Those that have money*. Certain companies have money to invest – an insurance company, for instance, needs to invest and grow its premiums to hopefully cover any claims and leave a profit. Other companies are established solely to invest money – a pension fund, for example, needs to invest all the monies given to it by the public in order to give back more than the fund was given to invest when the pensioner wants the money back.

Merchant bank

A merchant bank's customers are also businesses. Historically, merchant banks facilitated trade between businesses – for example, they would allow a business to buy goods from an overseas business by guaranteeing the payments. Nowadays there is little distinction between merchant and investment banks, and more are known by the more modern description of investment bank.

The capital markets

Companies need cash to run their business: to buy machines and premises, to purchase raw materials, to pay wages. This cash is *capital*. The capital is typically raised in two ways: by the company selling part/all of itself to shareholders, or via some form of loan (or 'debt', as it is known). There are advantages and disadvantages to this.

Shares

Shares … stocks… equity … three names for the same thing. The company sells part/all of the ownership of itself. Advantages for the organisation raising the money are that there is no requirement to repay the cash or to pay interest. The downside is loss of ownership

– shareholders dictate the strategy ultimately and own their share of any profits.

Bonds

A bond is a loan. The investor lends the company money in return for a bond certificate, which details the terms of the loan – for example, a 30-year loan paying 5% interest per year. The advantage for the organisation raising the money is that there is no loss of ownership – it's a loan. Disadvantages are that it's a loan and, as such, must be repaid with interest. The interest payable will be dependent upon the view of the investors of the chances of getting their money back! For example, as I write this you can invest your savings with the U.K. government (HM Treasury) for five years at 3.9%. The chance of you getting your money back in five years from the U.K. government is virtually 100%. Now imagine there is a new start-up company 'Start-up Ltd' that wants to borrow your cash. Are you interested in lending to them at the same 3.9% rate for five years? I wouldn't be, because the probability of me getting my money back is far less than 100%, but I'm getting the same reward. For me to be enticed to lend to Start-up Ltd, I'd need a far better risk/reward payout. If Start-up Ltd was paying 10% on its bond, I could lend £100 and be paid £21 interest in two years. Lending that same £100 to HM treasury for 3.9% would only get me £21 interest after five years – taking three years more to earn the same return. So now Start-up Ltd has my attention! You can see that the 3.9% is a 'fixed' amount and that I will receive this each year – I will have an 'income'. This is why bonds are known as *fixed income.*

Primary markets

The first time new capital is raised in this way it is called *primary issuance*. Specifically, the primary issuance of shares is known as the IPO – initial public offering. Investment banks arrange capital-raising activities for their clients. This is known as *underwriting*, and in exchange for the fees the bank receives, it guarantees (underwrites) the issue. That is, if the shares/bonds do not sell, then the bank itself will buy them. The buyers or investors would be those mentioned previously: pension funds, investment funds, insurance companies and, ultimately, the public.

Trading

It would certainly be less attractive if those buyers felt they had to own the equity forever and own the bonds until they paid back in, for example, 30 years (the maturity). Who wants to invest in something you can't get out of? This brings us to the purpose of trading floors. They provide a market where you can sell these investments, maybe even back to the institution that was involved in their underwriting in the first place. They will also allow you to buy more shares/bonds already issued. This is called *secondary trading* – and this is what trading floors do in these capital markets. Most trading houses have equity and fixed income trading floors.

So what good does trading do?

- It provides a secondary market, without which companies would find it very difficult to raise capital, and ultimately, the whole economy would grind to a halt.
- It makes profits, and those profits are owned by the shareholders (not the traders). The shareholders will include pension funds and investment funds investing the public's money.

Trading floor roles

One of the main purposes of the floor is to buy/sell financial instruments (stocks, bonds, etc.) for the bank's clients. We call this *market-making*. Let's imagine that Start-up Ltd issues bonds that were bought by a pension fund. The pension fund bought them because its strategy was to invest a certain portion of its funds under management in a riskier product to enhance the returns for the pensioners. The pension fund will need to sell the bonds at some point, either to take a profit, stop a loss or to turn the bonds back into cash to pay the pensioners. When the pension fund wants to sell, it will contact several banks or securities firms (bonds and equities are securities) to get 'best execution' (the best combination of price and 'liquidity' – the ability to buy/sell the amount you need). This brings us to the first of the trading-floor roles.

Sales

The salesperson's role is to own the relationship with the client. Salespeople need to understand the requirements of their clients and to deliver the service they need, execution capability (the ability to rapidly buy and sell), research, etc. In our example, the pension fund would inform the salesperson that it either wanted to sell (we call this *showing your side*) or that it wanted the prices at which they could buy or sell (known as a *two-way* price). Declaring your intention (showing your side) will often get the customer the best price, as the bank knows what the customer needs to do and can work to that objective. The salesperson will then contact his or her trader in order to obtain this price.

Trading

The trader's task is to 'make a market' for the banks customers – to always be available to buy or sell from/to the customer. The trader will set the price according to where it can be bought/sold in the market, adjusted for his or her desire to win the trade. Some markets are physical locations where trading takes place (e.g., the London Metals Exchange), but nowadays most are not and 'the market' is simply the collective name for the traders at all other banks and securities houses. The London Stock Exchange, for example, closed its trading floor in the 1980s; trading on stocks is performed electronically by the banks and securities houses from their own locations.

Once the trader has determined the price at which it is willing to buy or sell, the trader informs the salesperson, who relays that to the customer. The customer has usually asked several institutions for a price and will execute the trade with whichever provides the best price and ability to execute the size of transaction. If the customer wishes to trade at the price given, the salesperson informs the trader, and the trader must then decide to either cover the position instantly with the market (i.e., buy or sell from another bank) or to hold the position in anticipation of the price becoming more favourable or because it suits the trader to cover positions currently in his or her trading book.

Operational risk

Operational risk is defined as 'the risk of direct or indirect loss resulting from inadequate or failed internal processes, people and systems or from external events'. It should be noted that 'reputational risk' is one potential outcome of operational risk but is excluded from the scope of this definition. Losses arising from strategic risk are not considered operational risk events.

Responsibilities

Operational risk management is everyone's responsibility and is performed at each level of the organisation, down to individual staff members. Generally, line managers are supported by dedicated operational risk (OpRisk) across a bank. Many divisions/departments have their own OpRisk teams, while other areas have OpRisk 'contacts' (i.e., OpRisk is a component of their job rather than all of it).

The industry standard for the operational risk policy is that a product/front-office COO's responsibilities would include:

- Providing information requested by the board for consolidated operational risk reporting.
- Escalating any operational risk issues to management as appropriate.
- Acting as a central point of contact on any operational risk issues in his or her department.
- Ensuring that the operational risk management framework is appropriately implemented in their department.

Principal OpRisk teams' interfaces are:

- The CRO division. It is responsible for setting a bankwide framework for the management of operational risk.
- Where appointed, control COOs/CCOs.
- Markets/IB/bank operations line control – the risk and control function with Operations.
- PC operational risk – product control's dedicated OpRisk function.

In-business COO/CCO (the Chief Control Officer*) OpRisk meetings – 1LOD (1st line of defence)

(Note: This area is further investigated in Maurice Evlyn-Bufton's follow-on boon, 'To Catch a Thief, the evolution of the Chief Control Officer'.)

This is an increasingly key governance process within the overall operational risk management infrastructure. It provides an opportunity for support departments to raise issues requiring management attention.

This process facilitates issue escalation/resolution and is a communication channel between the businesses (1LOD) and the support areas, operations, product control, compliance, operational risk (2LOD).

The main purpose of the CCO/1LOD function is to ensure key unmitigated risks/issue that warrant management attention are escalated and owned and subsequent actions agreed and monitored.

Why are CCOs so important?

In order to run a business line, there is a collective responsibility between front and back office (all support departments) to ensure that risks and issues are adequately managed. They provide an opportunity for front-office management to discuss developments with stakeholders. Support departments use this mechanism to ensure that the front office understands the key operational issues and risks and how they impact the ability to support the business. It ensures accountability is assigned for resolving issues and that any associated actions are tracked to completion.

Scope and business interface of the CCO

Primary:

- Head of business.
- Product COOs.
- Product control.
- Middle office/trade support.
- Operations.
- IT.
- Operational risk.
- Compliance.

Secondary:

- Credit risk management.
- New business.
- Internal audit.
- Financial accounting.
- Tax.
- Treasury.
- Human resources.
- Operational risk.
- Business continuity management.
- Client account solutions.

Product definitions

Bonds

These are capital market instruments issued by borrowers to investors. With most bonds, the borrower pays interest by means of an annual or semi-annual coupon and returns the funds to the investor at the pre-agreed maturity of the bond. The major bond issuers are governments and companies, with individual bond issues having a size ranging from a few tens of million U.S. dollars up to several billion. Within the market there are many variations of bond: zero coupon, convertible, callable, putable, perpetual.

Commodities

Many have argued that commodities are the basis of the modern economy. Energy, metals and agriculture are the prime examples. It is certain that these products are very different from financial products; each is physical in nature, changes form as it is refined in some manner, and many are concentrated in geographic areas that can be regarded as less stable politically.

Credit products

Credit risk refers to the situation where a lender does not receive either interest or principal from a borrower. Credit products provide a lender with the opportunity to purchase something very similar to insurance against this risk. The major product is the credit default swap, which can be traded on all major corporate and government borrowers throughout the globe. Other credit products include iTraxx and CDX index products where it is possible to trade credit insurance on 125 borrowers simultaneously.

DCM

This is the process by which new funds are raised by corporate customers. Banks advise on the most efficient way to borrow, through either loans or bonds. These transactions may follow from merger, leverage buyout or other major corporate restructuring where the bank will be providing specialist financial advice.

Derivatives

The term derivative refers to financial instruments that derive price and risk characteristics from other instruments, such as shares. Futures are traded on recognised financial exchanges, whereby buyer and seller agree to exchange a specified quantity and quality of an asset at an agreed price at an agreed date in the future. Interest rate swaps are agreements whereby counterparties exchange fixed and variable interest payments on agreed dates. Options are agreements where the owner can choose to buy (or sell) an asset at an agreed price on an agreed date in the future, if it is economically sensible to do so.

FX (foreign exchange)

Exchanging one currency for another is the essence of an FX transaction. In terms of volume traded, the global FX market is the largest financial market in the world. Some of this volume is related to trade flows, but much is generated by the speculative community.

Life of a trade

This is how a transaction flows through the bank: customer enquiry, pricing and risk analysis, execution, information flow between departments, documentation and settlement. All areas and departments within the bank will be studied to see how information pertaining to the transaction is used.

Mortgages

The major financial transaction for most individuals, mortgages allow borrowing secured against a property. There are many variations available – for example fixed or floating interest rate, payments including capital repayment or interest only, the requirement for the lender to provide lower interest rates if market rates move. Groups of individual mortgages can be bundled together and repackaged as mortgaged bonds.

Structured notes

Institutional investors and private bank customers are often limited by regulations in the scope of financial products that are permissible for investment – namely cash, shares and bonds. Structured notes have cash flow profiles that are very similar to bonds. The exact profile depends on the instruments that have been embedded within the note. In essence these are products that allow for more varied investment, along with often providing the security of capital protection to the investor.

Syndicate

Banks work together to perform very large transactions on behalf of customers. These are often loans, where individual banks do not have the appetite for lending more than a proportion of the entire sum borrowed by a customer. In the new issue markets, banks help customers to raise funds by issuing new shares or bonds, which are sold through the sales force of the banks. The customer often looks for a syndicate of banks to work together for a more universal sales effort.

ABOUT GCF BOSNIA

Goražde Children's Foundation

GCF Bosnia is a UK-based charitable foundation committed to helping rejuvenate the previously war-torn town of Goražde in Bosnia. The charity specifically supports Goražde Primary School and seeks to provide a brighter future for its children.

To date, through the foundation's efforts, an English language teaching centre has been established, and the previously battle-scarred playground has been refurbished into an all-purpose playground pitch for the children to play sport. Future plans include the construction of a fully equipped science classroom.

GCF Bosnia was founded by Maurice Evlyn-Bufton, previously a captain in The 1st Battalion Royal Gloucestershire, Berkshire and Wiltshire Regiment (1RGBW). He served with the battalion on United Nations' service, as part of its peacekeeping force during the Bosnian conflict (1992–95) and is currently Managing Director of executive search company Armstrong Wolfe. The foundation was set up in memory of four of his comrades, who were killed whilst on operational service as part of the United Nations' deployment in Bosnia.

In the late summer of 1994, the newly formed Royal Gloucestershire, Berkshire and Wiltshire Regiment (RGBW) conducted its first operational tour. This was as part of the United

Nations Protection Force (UNPROFOR) – the first of three international missions that assisted in bringing peace and stability to this troubled part of the Balkans.

Battalion Tactical HQ, A and B Companies 1RGBW were based in Goražde, one of the three Bosnian Muslim eastern enclaves inside Bosnian Serb territory, south of Srebenica. Their mission was to protect the 60,000 Bosnian Muslim refugees from the Bosnian Serb Army besieging the town. For a number of reasons, due in no small part to UN military intervention, it did not suffer the fate of its neighbours Srebrenica and Zepa. After the fall of these towns, Goražde became the last Muslim enclave in eastern Bosnia.

Defended by UN forces throughout 1994–95, it was not until the ceasefire and Dayton Accord that the roads from Goražde to Sarajevo were opened to civilian and UN traffic. Conditions in Goražde had been harsh, bearing the scars of years of a bitter struggle. Tragically, during this tour, in September 1994, Privates Ben Hinton, Philip Armstrong, Martin Dowdell and Chris Turner were killed in two separate incidents. In addition, a number of 1RGBW and Corps attached soldiers were injured and have suffered both short-term and long-term medical and mental effects.

In 2012, 17 former comrades of 1RGBW returned to Goražde to replace the memorial stones to their fallen comrades, this time dedicated by the battalion's 1994 padre, Patrick Irwin, and the Reverend Andrew Grant. Andrew was a private soldier in 1RGBW in 1994 and was involved in one of the incidents. At this moment he experienced an epiphany and some years later was ordained in York Minster. On the last day of this visit, the group was invited to the local primary school and was surprised by the children singing them a song in Bosnian, thanking the British Army for saving their parents and grandparents.

Moved and inspired by this gesture, Maurice asked the school's headmistress what he could do to help. From this discussion was

born a commitment to establish an English language teaching centre and to re-establish a playing field, both in memory of their fallen comrades and as an investment that would benefit the future generations of Goražde, the Bosnian town the soldiers of 1RGBW had defended many years before.

Through his company Armstrong Wolfe, Maurice has raised over £30,000 to help fund the school's ambitions and set up the Goražde Children's Foundation to manage these donations. In addition to various fundraising activities, in March 2015 Maurice and a number of employees from Armstrong Wolfe ran a marathon starting on hills above Goražde, to be welcomed by the children cheering them as they crossed the bridge that took them over the river Drina and back to the school. Maurice has now committed to providing a new science laboratory to sit alongside the English speaking laboratory, which he hopes will be a benefit to the young children of Goražde.

For more information, go to www.gcfbosnia.org

ABOUT SIGHTSAVERS

Sightsavers

Introducing Sightsavers

Sightsavers is an international development organisation focused on eliminating avoidable blindness and ensuring equality for people with disabilities in developing countries. We believe that no one should be blind from avoidable causes, and that people whose sight can't be saved should live with dignity and independence. Sightsavers works with local partners, focusing on those living in poverty in over 30 of the poorest countries in Africa and Asia.

Eye health

Globally, over 285 million people are visually impaired, including 39 million blind people . Ninety per cent of those affected live in developing countries, and an incredible 80 per cent of all visual impairment is known to be preventable or curable . People affected by visual impairments are far more likely to experience lower incomes, unemployment, hunger, a lack of access to health services and exclusion from education and society.

Sightsavers supports and strengthens local eye care systems to tackle preventable blindness. We provide specialist training for health care professionals, increase public awareness of eye care and lobby governments to ensure it is universally available as an integral part of wider health care systems.

Working with partners in developing countries, we restore sight or prevent blindness for millions of people each year; from conditions such as cataracts, the leading cause of avoidable blindness, to river blindness and trachoma, two blinding neglected tropical diseases. Treatments for these conditions are inexpensive yet life changing; from just 7p to prevent or treat someone suffering with river blindness or 35p to prevent or treat trachoma, to a sight-restoring cataract operation costing just £28.

The impacts of these straight-forward treatments are enormous; for example cataract surgery can lead to increased economic productivity in the first year equivalent to 1,500% of the cost of the treatment itself . In 2015 Sightsavers supported over 70 million treatments to protect against blinding neglected tropical disease, and carried out over 255,000 operations to restore sight or prevent blindness.

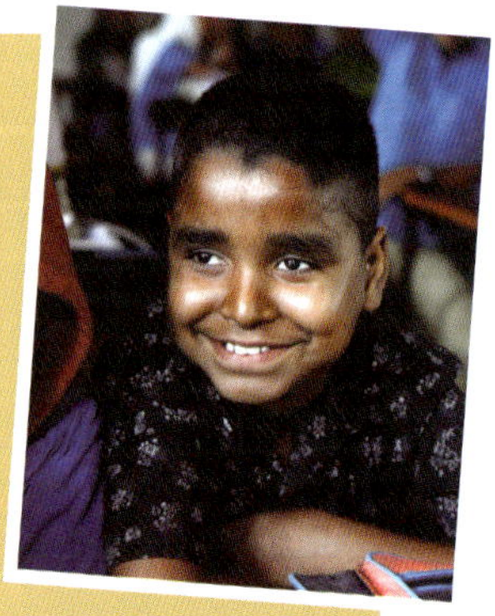

Before Ranin (right) had even turned one, he was diagnosed with cataracts in his left eye. His parents were told that he would lose his sight if an operation didn't take place, but the cost of the operation was too much for them to afford.

Fortunately, Ranin was identified by a health worker trained in eye care under Sightsavers' programme in Bangladesh. His cataract was re-diagnosed and, as his family could not afford to pay, he received surgery free of charge. Following his surgery, Ranin is now a happy and playful boy, looking forward to playing cricket in the future.

Education and social inclusion

Sightsavers works to make sure disabled adults and children have the same rights and opportunities as everyone else, being treated as equal members of society. We believe that access to education is invaluable in helping people to escape poverty, and we work to make sure children with visual impairments and other disabilities get the chance to go to school.

Over a billion people worldwide live with some form of disability. In the developing countries where we work, people with disabilities such as blindness are often isolated and excluded from their communities. They typically have poorer health, lower educational achievements and higher rates of poverty. The opportunities for children with disabilities to gain an education are dramatically reduced, as they constitute more than one-third of the 57 million primary school age children not currently enrolled in primary school . In Africa in particular, less than ten per cent of disabled children attend primary school .

Sightsavers supports the principle of inclusive education; ensuring that all pupils, including those with disabilities, participate equally and learn together effectively. This teaches them from an early age that they are all equal and valued members of society. We run projects that deliver high quality education for children with visual impairments and other disabilities in their local schools. These projects are both scalable and cost effective, allowing us to also use them as examples to lobby governments for change, ensuring that many more children with disabilities can access an education alongside their peers.

We also provide life skills and vocational training for both young people and adults with disabilities, supporting the formation of self-help groups and helping those groups to make the voices of their members heard by those making the decisions that affect them. Alongside this we directly lobby governments to fulfil their obligations under international conventions for disabled people.

In 2015 we supported more than 3,600 children with disabilities to gain a mainstream education, and provided life skills and vocational training for more than 16,000 people with visual impairments and other disabilities.

Gideon (left) is one of the students supported through Sightsavers inclusive education programme in Kenya. He was born completely blind and his parents had little hope of his gaining an education and independence, as the only school they knew of in Kenya that catered for the blind was in Thika, 350 kilometres away.

Fortunately, a local social worker told Gideon's parents about Sightsavers' recently established inclusive education programme in their area. He was referred to the programme and then placed at Korara Primary School where he began learning alongside his sighted peers. Gideon proved himself to be both a bright student and talented musician, and in 2013 he gained his certificate of primary education, progressing to secondary school.

ABOUT ST. GEORGE'S SOCIETY OF NEW YORK

ST GEORGE'S SOCIETY OF NEW YORK

Patron: HRH The Duke of Gloucester KG GCVO

St. George's Society of New York (founded in 1770) is a membership organisation with a charitable purpose. It provides vital assistance to people of British and Commonwealth heritage in New York who are in need of financial and emotional support. For example the sick, elderly and disabled and students who have the ability to succeed but lack the funds to complete their studies. The Society's vibrant network of influential people and partnerships with key organisations in the British community make it the pre-eminent Anglo/American social and philanthropic group in the tristate area.

Beneficiary Program

Each year, with the generous support of its community, the Society is able to prevent seniors from losing their homes. Many of the St. George's beneficiaries are referred from housing court in a desperate attempt to stop an eviction. For these people, once they retired, they faced the struggle that their income was not sufficient to pay their rent so once all savings were depleted, the terrifying prospect of losing their homes becomes real. Most are unable to work and so without financial assistance, they could indeed be forced into homelessness.

In addition to rent support, the Society provides help with home care expenses, medication, utilities and other quality of life supports. While financial assistance is critical, the St. George's Society's two dedicated social workers also offer much-needed emotional support.

"When I was diagnosed with cancer I struggled with the daily dilemma of whether to pay for medical supplies essential for my care or my housing costs. Thanks to St. George's Society, now I can focus on treatment and getting better without the worry of losing my home."

ENID FROM THE UNITED KINGDOM
ST. GEORGE'S SOCIETY BENEFICIARY

Scholarship Program

St. George's Society assists British and Commonwealth students who have achieved excellent academic standing in their first three years but due to financial hardship are unable to complete their final year of undergraduate studies. Since 2008, the Society has awarded over $700,000 in scholarships to hundreds of students at Lehman College in the Bronx. Many of the Society's scholars aspire to pursue careers in health services, nursing, education and other professions that give back to the community.

"Thanks to the St. George's Society scholarship I have been able to invest time in studying, volunteering and internships in order to complete my Bachelor's degree in Biology. My dream

is to become a cancer specialist and I look forward to taking the medical college admission test this fall and moving closer to making my dream a reality."

KASHFIA FROM BANGLADESH
ST. GEORGE'S SOCIETY SCHOLAR

Medical and Emergency Relief

In addition to the Society's beneficiary and scholarship programs, they also respond to appeals for emergency assistance, for people who are facing medical crises. In January 2015, the Society assisted a British couple who were visiting New York when their baby boy arrived 11 weeks early weighing just 3.4lbs. The new parents were stranded in America for several weeks while baby Dax was monitored in a Neonatal Intensive Care Unit at Lenox Hill. St. George's Society provided funds to cover food, transportation and incidentals. The Society also offered guidance and paid the application fees for the newborn's passport to enable him to travel back to the UK once he met the minimum weight requirement and was able to breathe and feed on his own.

"When I gave birth to Dax prematurely, it was the hardest thing we have ever faced. Without St. George's it would have been very difficult to cope. They were a massive help and a huge shoulder when we needed it the most."

KATIE, DAX'S MOTHER

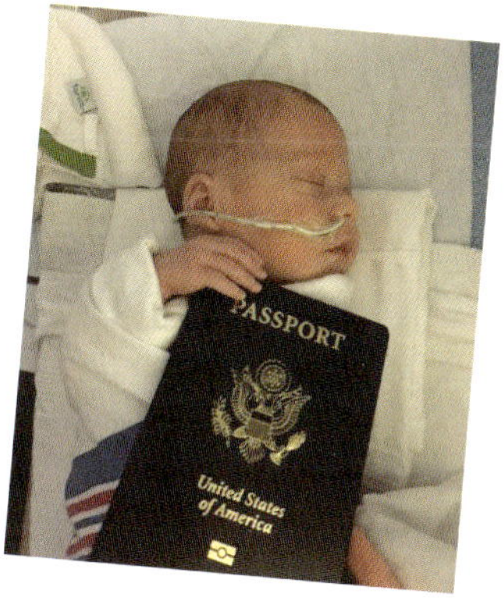

These are just a few examples of the life-changing assistance that St. George's Society provides to people in desperate need thanks to the support of its members and friends.

You can join today or donate online at
www.stgeorgessociety.org
St. George's Society of New York
216 East 45th Street, Suite 901
New York, New York 10017
212 682 6110

St. George's Society of New York is a registered non-profit 501 (c) (3) organization. Tax ID: 23-7426425. The Society receives no government funding and its charitable programs are primarily funded by membership dues, donations and events.